Yale Univer      *FA*

nent

ardi
The Intertek Group

Petter N. Kolm
Yale University

Trends in Quantitative Finance

RESEARCH FOUNDATION
OF CFA INSTITUTE

Statement of Purpose

The Research Foundation of CFA Institute is a not-for-profit organization established to promote the development and dissemination of relevant research for investment practitioners worldwide.

ISBN 978-1-932495-49-2

Printed in the United States of America

21 April 2006

Editorial Staff

Elizabeth A. Collins
Book Editor

David L. Hess
Assistant Editor

Kara H. Morris
Production Manager

Lois Carrier
Production Specialist

Biographies

Frank J. Fabozzi, CFA, CPA, is adjunct professor of finance and Becton Fellow in the School of Management at Yale University and editor of the *Journal of Portfolio Management.* Prior to joining the Yale faculty, he was a visiting professor of finance in the Sloan School at the Massachusetts Institute of Technology. Professor Fabozzi is on the advisory council for the Department of Operations Research and Financial Engineering at Princeton University and has authored and edited numerous books in finance. In 2002, he was inducted into the Fixed Income Analysts Society's Hall of Fame. Professor Fabozzi holds a doctorate in economics from the City University of New York.

Sergio M. Focardi is a founding partner of the Paris-based consulting firm The Intertek Group. Mr. Focardi lectures at the Center for Interdisciplinary Research in Economics and Finance at the University of Genoa (Italy) and is a member of the editorial board of the *Journal of Portfolio Management.* He has written numerous articles on econophysics and is the coauthor of *Modeling the Markets: New Theories and Techniques; Risk Management: Framework, Methods and Practice; The Mathematics of Financial Modeling and Investment Management;* and *Financial Modeling of the Equity Markets: From CAPM to Cointegration.* Mr. Focardi holds a degree in electronic engineering from the University of Genoa and a postgraduate degree in communications from the Galileo Ferraris Electrotechnical Institute, Turin, Italy.

Petter N. Kolm is a doctoral student in finance at the School of Management, Yale University, and a financial consultant in New York City. Previously, he worked in the Quantitative Strategies group at Goldman Sachs Asset Management, where his responsibilities included research and development of new quantitative investment strategies for the group's hedge fund. Dr. Kolm is a member of the editorial board of the *Journal of Portfolio Management* and is a coauthor of *Financial Modeling of the Equity Markets: From CAPM to Cointegration.* He holds a doctorate in mathematics from Yale University, an MPhil in applied mathematics from the Royal Institute of Technology in Stockholm, and an MS in mathematics from ETH Zurich.

Contents

PROFESSIONAL
DEVELOPMENT
QUALIFIED ACTIVITY

This publication qualifies for 5 PD credits under the guidelines
of the CFA Institute Professional Development Program.

Foreword

Mark Kritzman, CFA, my predecessor as research director at the Research Foundation of CFA Institute, is a wit as well as an intellect and once referred to those casually acquainted with quantitative finance as "dilequants" (rhymes with dilettantes). If you dabble in quantitative methods and wonder whether you might be so characterized, you shouldn't be insulted. I'm a dilequant too. Understanding and applying quantitative techniques in finance takes a lifetime of study and mastery, and most practitioners would do well to strive for understanding what quantitative methods in finance are, and what they are best used for, rather than trying to achieve this mastery on their own.

But for quantitative methods to be used and appreciated in the investment community, one needs a primer on the topic for a nontechnical audience. The current monograph achieves this difficult goal. Its authors, Frank J. Fabozzi, CFA, Sergio M. Focardi, and Petter N. Kolm, have translated the often highly technical jargon and mathematical language used by "quants" into plain English.

Quantitative finance is broadly applied in three areas: (1) screening universes of securities to help select those one wants to buy (or sell short) in an effort to add alpha relative to a benchmark, (2) portfolio construction, in which optimization and related methods are used to build efficient portfolios of those securities, and (3) pricing derivatives.

The current monograph focuses, strongly but not exclusively, on portfolio construction. Fabozzi, Focardi, and Kolm pay considerable attention to optimization in the presence of estimation error, a topic raised most visibly by Richard Michaud in his January/February 1989 *Financial Analysts Journal* article, "The Markowitz Optimization Enigma: Is 'Optimized' Optimal?" Approaching the problem from a different angle, Fischer Black and Robert Litterman, in their September/October 1992 *Financial Analysts Journal* article "Global Portfolio Optimization," also addressed the issue of estimation uncertainty in portfolio construction, as did J. David Jobson and Bob Korkie in a series of articles in the early 1980s. Fabozzi, Focardi, and Kolm expand on all of these concerns. And increased interest in alternative assets, such as hedge funds, for which the standard assumption of a normal distribution of returns may not apply, creates a need for "robust" optimization methods, to which the authors of this monograph devote considerable attention.

Another topic addressed by Fabozzi, Focardi, and Kolm is the use of advanced econometric techniques to try to add alpha by forecasting security (or asset-class) returns. Although the standard assumptions of portfolio theory—the efficient market hypothesis, the no-arbitrage condition, and general equilibrium models of asset pricing, such as the capital asset pricing model—posit a world in which returns are not forecastable, these assumptions do not always hold up. Practitioners have made money by forecasting. The current monograph provides a primer on some of the more widely used forecasting techniques by covering such important issues as model selection, biases in models, and data mining and snooping.

Finally, in an innovative section, the authors provide results of a survey in which investment management organizations reveal what quantitative techniques they use and what challenges they face in using them.

In summary, Fabozzi, Focardi, and Kolm provide an excellent and comprehensive survey of the challenges one meets in using quantitative methods for portfolio construction and forecasting. By covering a wide variety of methods rather than advocating a particular one, the monograph reflects an inclusive and thoughtful approach.

The Research Foundation is very pleased to present *Trends in Quantitative Finance*.

Laurence B. Siegel
Research Director
The Research Foundation of CFA Institute

Introduction

The aim of this monograph is to introduce practitioners to recent developments in the modeling of equity returns for the purpose of asset management. We have tried to provide a plain-English, formula-free review of quantitative methods without sacrificing conceptual rigor. In addition to discussing methodology, the monograph includes the results of an *ad hoc* survey taken in the first half of 2005 of equity modeling at 21 large asset management firms in the United States and Europe.

As a profession, asset managers have traditionally tried to "beat the market"—that is, to earn returns in excess of returns obtained by an indexed strategy. Their ability (real or supposed) to construct portfolios that earn excess returns is the reason investors entrust assets to them and the justification for active management fees in excess of index fund fees. This effort to outperform the market is one reason for the growing use of modeling techniques in asset management.

Market Efficiency and Unpredictability

Under the assumption that modern financial markets are efficient, mainstream finance theory has traditionally held that markets cannot be beaten. Although excess returns might indeed be achieved, they are considered to be, on average, proportional to risk: Markets embed a risk–return trade-off in which investors demand, and markets supply, excess expected returns for taking risk. In an efficient market, the risk–return trade-off also implies that above-market returns cannot be achieved without taking additional risk.

The assumption of market efficiency is associated with the notion of the *unpredictability* of financial markets. Mainstream theory maintains that markets must be unpredictable because if markets were predictable, they could not be efficient and returns in excess of market returns could be made without taking additional risk.

The notion of market efficiency has given rise to "passive" asset management strategies because if markets are efficient, trying to beat the market is futile. Better to reduce management costs by investing so as to match the performance of broad indices.

Given the double-digit returns that the U.S. equity markets were providing in the last two decades of the 20th century, few practitioners were overly concerned about the debate on market efficiency. As the 1990s drew to a close, however, the academic view of market efficiency and market predictability began to change under the weight of empirical evidence and fresh theoretical insights. The market downturn after 2000 forced asset management firms to reevaluate their investment processes in an effort to reduce costs and produce returns in unrewarding markets. Because quantitative methods can help in both tasks, many firms began to take a closer look at these methodologies.

Actually, a complete conceptual overhaul of our thinking about equity price processes is needed. The practice of investment management has to be reconciled with a new theoretical concept of asset returns—namely, that the trade-off between risk and return is dynamic and does not exclude the possibility that asset returns are, to some extent, forecastable. This monograph provides an overview of the recent changes in finance theory and the modeling techniques that the industry is using or beginning to experiment with in an attempt to capture the limited forecastability in financial markets.

New Concepts of Risk and Return

The only really general observation we can make about market efficiency is the absence of arbitrage—that is, in the financial markets, one cannot make a sure profit with no net investment. There is no free lunch. Pragmatically, therefore, whatever strategy investors adopt, they always face the possibility of losing money. Although finance theory states that investors (or asset managers) cannot beat the market without risk (because doing so would entail arbitrage), it does admit that an investor can beat the market, on average, by taking risk beyond the risk inherent in the market benchmark. Taking this additional risk means, of course, that the investor will suffer periods of underperformance as well as periods of superior performance relative to the market benchmark.

To make the critical decisions about how much risk to take, the profession clearly needs a quantitative framework for measuring risk and return—which is provided by probability theory and statistical techniques. The quantitative principles of investment under uncertainty were laid down by Markowitz (1952) more than 50 years ago; their adoption in full earnest requires the use of quantitative methods and modeling. But even today, the adoption of these techniques by the asset management community is patchy.

In a probabilistic quantitative framework, a number of concepts about markets have to be critically revised. Market efficiency does not imply that all investments are equivalent: Given one's risk–return preferences, some investments are preferable to others. Thus, we cannot state that all excess returns are equally offset by risk to the point where every investment has the same certainty-equivalent return. Some returns are less offset by risk than others. What remains true is that without investment and risk, one cannot make money. Equivalently, one cannot always, or even usually, beat the market.

To measure the ability of a manager to engineer a favorable risk–return trade-off, researchers introduced the concepts of *beta* (a measure of exposure to market risk) and *alpha* (a measure of return in excess of the market return, which can be interpreted as measuring skill in stock picking or asset allocation). All security or portfolio returns comprise a market part (beta) and a nonmarket part (alpha). The beta part of the return is caused by correlation with the relevant market benchmark and thus arises from market exposure, not active management. The alpha part is the return "above and beyond" the beta part and represents the value added by the active manager.

Note explicitly that many realizations of asset management strategies will show positive alpha *ex post*. The key challenge of investment management, however, is to identify *ex ante* which strategies will produce positive alpha. Having generated a positive alpha *ex post* is not by itself a sign of a good active strategy: Such a result can sometimes be achieved simply by luck. Strategies can be considered alpha generators only if alphas are persistent. For this reason, performance measurement is a delicate issue. Because we cannot rely on always having access to long series of past performance, we try to gauge the true performance of an asset manager by correcting his *ex post* performance with an estimate of the risk associated with his strategy.

Models of equity returns can be static or dynamic. The models of standard finance are static; that is, the distributions of the model variables do not depend on the previous path of the same variables. A random walk is a typical example of a static model. Consequently, from the point of view of standard finance, alphas and betas are interpreted as static terms; they are constants that do not change over time.

However, we can also model the market with dynamic models. In these models, the variables do depend on their previous paths. If we use dynamic models, the concepts of alpha and beta have to be reinterpreted. In fact, in linear dynamic models, we typically find long-term equilibrium relationships plus short-term dynamics. The implication is that alpha and beta change over time. Moreover, if we add nonlinearities and higher statistical moments (such as skewness or kurtosis) or nonnormal distributions, we find that the risk–return trade-offs of assets cannot be described by the linear relationship implied by alpha and beta.

Dynamic models entail predictability of expected returns or of higher moments. This predictability is compatible with finance theory if it generates no arbitrage opportunities. And keep in mind that forecasting models do not necessarily offer better risk–return trade-offs than static models without predictability. True static alpha, if it exists, generates abnormal profits without the trading costs associated with dynamic strategies.

Generally speaking, given the large universe of investable stocks, capturing market opportunities requires optimization methodologies to fully exploit the risk–return trade-offs that modeling allows us to identify. Entrusting the management of large sums to automatic models and optimizers entails a high level of confidence in models, however, so the robustness of the quantitative models (that is, their relative insensitivity to a violation of one or more assumptions) has become an important concern for many firms.

A central theme of this monograph is the trade-offs that must be made among model complexity, model risk, and model performance. We return to this idea time and again—particularly in Chapter 3 on robust methods, Chapter 6 on machine learning, Chapter 7 on model selection, and Chapter 9 on model estimation.

Overview of the Monograph

The 12 chapters of this monograph develop the themes we have outlined. We begin by analyzing the concept of forecastability. We discuss the difficulty in predicting financial markets because the predictions themselves influence (modify) market behavior. This phenomenon, known as "self-referentiality," does not mean that forecasting markets is impossible, only that there are constraints on the risk–return trade-offs offered by financial markets.

We argue that, counter to intuition, financial markets cannot be completely unpredictable yet at the same time contain a risk–return structure. If markets were totally unpredictable, for risk to be rewarded, they would have to exhibit different time-invariant expected returns. A static, immutable spread of returns between assets of different risk would lead to exponentially diverging prices and to exponentially diverging market capitalizations. This would occur whether stock returns provide alphas or not. Empirically, however, we do not find an exponential distribution of market capitalizations.[1] This observation leads to the conclusion that there is some forecastability in markets.

The idea that financial markets have some degree of forecastability has now gained broad acceptance. However, predictability is not automatically a source of profitability. We close Chapter 1 with a discussion of the need to carefully evaluate (1) the risk–return trade-off implied by the models and (2) transaction costs so as to ensure that strategies that look profitable on paper do not end up producing losses and/or inferior performance relative to a benchmark when applied in practice.

In Chapter 2, we outline the basic principles of general equilibrium theories. The objective is to improve understanding of the capital asset pricing model and the notion of market equilibrium. We then introduce the concept of the utility function, which represents the investor's financial decision-making processes. The utility function has proved to be an important concept for the practice as well as the theory of finance. In fact, every optimization process depends on the specification of a utility function.

Despite their theoretical weight, *general equilibrium* theories are difficult to test and to use in practice. The reason is that the specification of the utility function remains abstract; it is an *a priori* assumption, one not based on empirical investigation. In the absence of an independent empirical evaluation of utility functions, general equilibrium is a theoretical framework that can always be used insofar as, in the absence of arbitrage, any price process can be rationalized as a general equilibrium.

---

[1]Actually, we do find empirically that market capitalization follows a Pareto law. This Pareto law can be described intuitively by one of its properties: The size of an individual is inversely proportional to its rank. That is, the size of the second largest company is one-half the size of the biggest company, the third largest is one-third, and so on. Many phenomena, including economic phenomena, obey Pareto's laws.

In Chapter 3, we describe the modern robust framework for Markowitz mean–variance optimization. We begin by describing the essentials of mean–variance optimization theory.

One critical aspect of the theory is the estimation of the variance–covariance matrix. Because in estimating the variance–covariance matrix the number of entries grows with the square of the number of assets that are candidates for portfolio inclusion, the matrix becomes rapidly unmanageable. We discuss robust estimation methods that allow one to reduce the number of independent covariance entries to be estimated.

A second critical component of the modern framework for Markowitz mean–variance estimation is *robust optimization*. Introduced recently in finance and still a subject of research, robust optimization places constraints on the results of the optimization process as a function of the uncertainty associated with parameter estimation. We discuss how robust estimation and robust optimization are two integrated aspects of robust methodologies.

In Chapter 4, we begin to explore models that detect forecastability in asset returns. We discuss the types of delayed responses that markets can exhibit to past values of variables, such as prices or returns. Forecastability is thus exploited by strategies based on momentum, reversal, co-integration, and mean reversion. We then discuss the issue of model complexity and sample size—that is, the size of the available historical dataset. There is a relationship between the size of the sample used for estimation and the complexity of the models we can estimate. If the sample is large, we can estimate a complex model; otherwise, we can estimate only the essentials.

In Chapter 5, we review issues related to modeling at different time horizons. Most models currently in use are estimated and reestimated on moving "windows" of historical data. We discuss the conditions that allow the estimation of slowly changing models and models that exhibit sudden regime shifts. Then, we discuss the behavior of stock markets at long time horizons and the concept of time diversification (i.e., the concept that financial risk is statistically smaller in the long run than in the short run because the ups and downs tend to offset each other, on average).

In Chapter 6, we provide an overview of *machine learning* and its applications in finance. Machine learning is a universal modeling strategy that does not depend on any domain-specific theory. Therefore, when applied to finance, the models do not use finance theory but rely on purely statistical analysis of financial phenomena. Machine-learning methods place constraints on model complexity to ensure that they retain some forecasting capability. We discuss a number of specific techniques, including neural networks, decision trees, clustering, genetic algorithms, and support vector machines. We also provide a perspective on artificial intelligence and techniques for handling unstructured (e.g., textual) data and text-related technologies.

In Chapter 7, we review the process of model selection and its pitfalls. We discuss how to deal with *data snooping* and avoid *survivor biases*. We also cover risk mitigation in modeling and, extending the discussion begun in Chapter 4, consider model complexity and the size of sample data.

Chapter 8 offers an overview of models used in equity return forecasting. Among the families of models discussed are the widely used models that regress returns on predictors and models that exploit momentum and reversal phenomena. We also discuss complex models that, although not widely used in asset management today, are beginning to make their way into practice. Among these are autoregressive models, factor models, hidden-variable models, and regime-switching models.

Model estimation is the subject of Chapter 9. Although (in keeping with the nature of this monograph) this chapter does not contain formulas, it does provide an overview of the concept of estimation and of the sampling distribution. We then present the most widely used estimation methods: the least-squares method, the maximum-likelihood estimation method, and the Bayesian estimation method. The chapter closes with a description of the estimation of regressions and other related models introduced in previous chapters.

Optimization, and in particular robust optimization, is becoming an important component in portfolio management applications. Chapter 10 presents the conceptual framework of optimization and gives practical suggestions for implementation and software selection. The development of robust methods for estimation and optimization is one of the major achievements of modern financial modeling. Robust technologies assume that models and the inputs themselves (like humans) are uncertain; they evaluate the consequences of errors in the models and introduce corrections that mitigate the potentially negative effects of model and estimation errors.

One of the objectives of this monograph is to provide a reading of how quantitative methods are making their way into the investment management process. Chapter 11 presents the results of an *ad hoc* market survey covering the use of quantitative methods in three areas: equity return forecasting, model risk mitigation, and optimization. Twenty-one asset management firms in the United States and Europe shared information on what modeling approaches they are actually using and experimenting with. Survey results are discussed and summarized in a table.

Finally, Chapter 12 considers the state of quantitative modeling today, with a discussion of modeling for portfolio management and for the profession in general, and suggests some possible future developments.

Acknowledgments

We wish to express our appreciation to the Research Foundation of CFA Institute for funding this project and providing us with guidance in preparing the manuscript. Mark Kritzman, CFA, then chair of the Research Foundation, first suggested this project to us after reading some of our earlier research and reviewed several of the earlier chapters. Laurence Siegel who replaced him as chair of the Research Foundation, made helpful suggestions on the first draft of the manuscript. We also received insightful comments from Dennis McLeavey, CFA, of CFA Institute and Peter Bernstein.

1. Forecasting Financial Markets

Why are financial markets so difficult to predict? The short answer is that financial markets are difficult to predict because predictions influence markets themselves. Because predictions are potential sources of profits or losses, they produce market movements that provoke *immediate* changes in prices, thereby invalidating the predictions themselves. This consideration leads to the concept of market efficiency: An efficient market is a market where all new information about the future behavior of prices is immediately reflected in the prices themselves. An efficient market exploits all information. Financial predictions are inherently different from, say, weather predictions. Weather forecasts are "objective," in that they do not influence the weather itself.

The concept of market efficiency has been much debated. To gain a working understanding of market efficiency, we have to first abandon the notions of perfect forecasts and perfect efficiency that create conceptual difficulties. More pragmatically, we have to discuss the consequences of our ability to make forecasts, albeit imperfect ones. From the point of view of a practitioner, the counterintuitive aspect of market efficiency is the fact that the more efficient we are in gathering, analyzing, and acting upon information about markets and publicly traded companies, the less predictable markets are. Thus, one might conclude that investing in market analysis is useless. The solution of this apparent puzzle is that market predictability does exist but is limited. In addition, even in the absence of predictability, one needs to determine the risk–return profile of the assets. This chapter will discuss the trade-off that markets must offer in terms of predictability. We will discuss how complete absence of market predictability is economic nonsense but, at the same time, market predictability must be limited.

There is another important point that we will discuss: information. Much of finance theory is centered on the notion of information and information differentials. Intuitively, information is what we know. There is an information differential if some people know something that others do not know. For example, the financial statements of a corporation are information. It is a financial truism that information differentials lead to sources of profit. Insider trading is the typical example of exploiting an information differential. Leinweber (2003) recalled how in 1790 George Washington decided not to default on national debts and dispatched messengers from New York to spread the good news. A number of Wall Street investors saddled faster horses than Washington's messengers and bought as much debt as they could find at a very low price, thus making a huge profit. Recently, efforts have been made to ensure that information is disseminated simultaneously to all market participants. Technology has been helpful in this, although it has created new opportunities for dissemination of false information as described in Leinweber and Madhavan (2001).

If information were always certain, there would not be much to say from the conceptual point of view except, perhaps, a discussion of the technologies for making information available to market participants. However, information is uncertain: This fact creates a conceptual problem. In fact, finance theory has to take into consideration not only raw information but also the way (and speed) in which information is processed and interpreted by market participants. Two market participants might have the same raw information but different forecasting capability.

An understanding of the behavior of markets calls for an understanding of how market participants process historical information—uncertain in itself[1]—and make forecasts. Predictability is associated with information. Markets are said to be forecastable if forecasts depend on the past and present information. However, it should be remarked that lack of predictability does not mean absence of information. Because markets identify a risk–return trade-off even if there is no market forecastability, the ability to quantify a constant expected return and the associated constant risk implies that we possess a lot of information on markets even in the absence of forecastability.

This chapter discusses just what information there is in financial markets and why financial markets, although difficult to predict, nevertheless exhibit some predictability. The objective is to provide a guide to model selection. We begin by introducing the concept of predictability and its pitfalls. In fact, the notion of market efficiency is rooted in the conceptual difficulties associated with making predictions on a system that can be influenced by the predictions themselves.

The Concept of Predictability

To predict (or forecast) is to form an expectation of what will happen in the future. The idea of predicting the future has always fascinated people and has been the subject, successively, of magic, philosophical enquiry, and scientific debate. Already in ancient times, it was clear that the notion of predicting the future is subject to potential inconsistencies. If, for example, we received a "credible" prediction that tomorrow we will have a car accident on our way to work, we might either decide to leave the car at home or be extra careful with our driving. In either case, our behavior will have been influenced by the prediction, thus potentially invalidating

---

[1]For example, the financial statements might include incomplete or false statements as recent corporate accounting scandals have demonstrated. We have to admit that we have only uncertain information about the past; there is much "hidden information" that we do not know.

the prediction. It is because of inconsistencies of this type that Samuelson (1965) and Fama (1965) arrived at the apparently paradoxical conclusion that "properly anticipated prices fluctuate randomly."

Already in classical Greece, there were two concepts of prediction: (1) scientific prediction based on laws of nature and (2) prediction of human affairs based on revealing Fate. The possibility of scientific prediction was largely a Greek discovery. The Greeks laid down the concepts of basic universal laws of Nature on which scientific prediction is still based.[2] As regards human affairs, the Greeks were aware of the contradictions inherent in predicting the future course of actions that can be influenced by the prediction itself.

The Greeks solved the problem in one of two ways. First, they made predictions difficult to obtain and cryptic. To obtain a prediction might mean traveling over long distances; predictions were delivered through ambiguous signs, such as the flight of birds or the rustling of leaves, or ambiguous language, such as the oracle at Delphi called the Pythia.[3] Second, they showed how predictions might come true through tortuous and unpredictable paths. Greek tragedy is characterized by plots that are based on the realization of predictions through an unpredictable chain of events, often the result of the will of a capricious god. The ancient Greeks understood the contradictions inherent in forecasting the behavior of intelligent, adaptive systems: The ability to forecast leads to a basic "efficiency" of intelligent behavior. The Greek notion of scientific forecasting was, however, different from ours.

Today, the notion of forecastability hinges on how we can forecast the future given what we know today. Forecasting is the relationship between present information and future events. Change the present state of affairs, and the forecast changes. However, the relationship between the present state of affairs and the future is fixed and immutable. The state of affairs known at a given date is called the *information set* known at that date. This is the notion of forecastability that academics and market practitioners espouse in theories of asset pricing. Prices or returns are said to be forecastable if the knowledge of the past influences our forecast of the future. For example, if the future returns of a company's stock depend on the value of a set of financial ratios of the same company, then those returns are predictable. If the future returns of that stock do not depend on any variable known today, then returns are unpredictable.

[2] Archimedes' "burning mirrors" were the byproduct of their knowledge of optics.

[3] The Pythia's predictions were often shrewdly phrased, which caused many supplicants to misinterpret the advice. The most famous case is the prediction given to Croesus, king of Lydia (approximately present-day Turkey). In 550 BC, Croesus was preparing to invade the Persian Empire when he queried the Delphian Pythia about the wisdom of an attack. The Pythia answered, "If Croesus goes to war, he will destroy a great empire." Encouraged by this response, Croesus invaded Persia. The Persians counterattacked, invaded Lydia, and captured Croesus. The dethroned king sent his iron chains to Delphi with the question, "Why did you lie to me?" The priestess answered that her prophecy had indeed been fulfilled: Croesus had destroyed a great empire—his own!

The forecastability of stock returns continues to be at the center of a heated debate. It is believed that (1) predictable processes allow investors (or asset managers on behalf of their clients) to earn excess returns whereas (2) unpredictable processes do not allow one to earn excess returns. Neither is necessarily true. Understanding why will shed some light on the crucial issues in modeling. In a nutshell: (1) predictable expectations do not necessarily mean profit if they are associated with unfavorable risk and (2) unpredictable expectations can be profitable if their expected value is favorable (positive alpha).

Most of our knowledge is uncertain; our forecasts are also uncertain.[4] The development of probability theory gave us the conceptual tools to represent and measure the level of uncertainty.[5] Probability theory assigns a number—the probability—to every possible event. This number, the probability, might be interpreted in one of two ways:

- The probability of an event is a *quantitative measure* of the strength of our beliefs that a particular event will happen, where 1 represents certainty;
- Probability is the *percentage of times* (i.e., frequency) that we observe a particular event in a large number of observations.

The second interpretation is the one normally used in econometrics and in science at large. When we make a probabilistic forecast of an event, we assess the percentage of times that we expect to observe that event.

Consider again the returns of a company's stock. Suppose that returns are unpredictable, in the sense that future returns do not depend on the current information set. This does not mean that future returns are completely uncertain, in the same sense in which the outcome of throwing a die is uncertain. Clearly, we cannot believe that every possible return on the stock is equally likely. First, given the finite nature of the economy, there are upper and lower bounds for real returns. More importantly, if we look at past price series, we observe a distribution of return values.

It is thus reasonable to assume that our uncertainty is embodied in a probability distribution of returns. Absence of predictability means that the distribution of future returns does not change as a function of the present information set. In particular, the distribution of future returns does not change as a function of the

---

[4]In classical science, forecasting was deterministic: The future course of affairs can be determined with arbitrary precision provided we know the present state with arbitrary precision. This view was forcefully expressed by the French mathematician and physicist Pierre Simon Laplace (1749–1827): A supernatural being who knows the position of every material particle with arbitrary precision and has unlimited computational power can forecast the entire future course of the universe. However, with the development of modern science, it has become progressively clear that deterministic sure forecasts—if they exist at all—are only a restricted part of our knowledge.

[5]Bernstein (1998) offers a lively account of the development of the concepts of risk and uncertainty from the beginning of civilization to modern risk management.

present and past values of prices and returns. Thus, the distribution of returns does not change with time.[6] We can, therefore, state that

1. a price or return process is predictable if its distributions depend on the present information set and

2. a price or return process is unpredictable if its distributions are time-invariant.

Are Returns Predictable?

Equipped with the concept of predictability that we have just defined, we can now discuss why prices and returns are difficult (or perhaps impossible) to predict. The key is that any prediction that might lead to a trading profit tends to make that profit disappear. Suppose that the price of a stock is predicted to increase significantly in the next five days. Clearly, a large price increase is a source of profit. As a consequence, if that prediction is widely shared, investors will rush to buy that stock. But the demand thus induced will make the stock's price rise immediately, thus eliminating the source of profit and invalidating the forecast.

If predictions of stock returns were *certain*, then simple arbitrage arguments would dictate that all stocks should have the same return. In fact, if stock returns could be predicted with certainty and if there were different returns, then investors would choose only those stocks with the highest returns.

Perhaps we should be clear about what we mean by "certain" predictions. A certain prediction is a prediction that leaves no doubt about what will happen. For example, U.S. Treasury zero-coupon securities (Treasury bills and Treasury strips) offer a *certain* prediction of returns until the maturity date of the security because the maturity value is guaranteed by the full faith and credit of the U.S. government. Any forecast that leaves open the possibility that market forces will alter the forecast cannot be considered a certain forecast.

Stock return forecasts are not certain; as we have seen, uncertain predictions are embodied in probability distributions. Suppose that we have a joint probability distribution of the returns of the universe of investable stocks. We will discuss the behavior of investors who face uncertain choices in detail in Chapter 2. Suffice it to note here that investors will decide the rebalancing of their portfolios as a function of their probabilistic predictions and their risk–return preferences. The problem we are discussing here is whether general considerations of market efficiency can determine the mathematical form of price or return processes. In particular, we are

---

[6]In principle, it could also depend on time deterministically, but this possibility is not realistic. It could also be subject to uncertainty. However, if uncertainty is itself independent of the present information set, the result is another independent probability distribution. For example, uncertainty relative to a normal (Gaussian) distribution produces a mixture of Gaussians, which is another distribution.

interested in understanding whether stock prices or returns are necessarily unpredictable. The problem discussed in the literature is expressed roughly as follows:

> Suppose that returns are a series of random variables. These series will be fully characterized by the joint distributions of returns at any given time *t* and at any given set of different times. Suppose that investors know these distributions and that investors select their portfolios according to specific rules that depend on these distributions. Can we determine the form of admissible processes, that is, of admissible distributions?

Ultimately, the objective in solving the above problem is to eschew models that allow unreasonable inferences. Historically, three solutions have been proposed:

1. Returns fluctuate randomly around a given mean (i.e., returns are multivariate random walks).
2. Returns are a fair game (i.e., returns are martingales).
3. Returns are a fair game after adjusting for risk.

These concepts and their differences will be explained in the following sections. The first two proposed solutions are incorrect; the last is too general to be useful for portfolio management. Before we discuss models of prices in more detail, we digress to provide some basic statistical concepts.

Concepts of Predictability and Unpredictability.
In this section, we define concepts of predictability and unpredictability that are important in financial modeling. We first define the concepts of strict white noise, a martingale difference sequence, and white noise:

- *Strict white noise* is a sequence of zero-mean, finite-variance independent and identically distributed (IID) variables, and it is thus unpredictable, in the sense that the conditional distribution of the variables is fixed and independent of the past. Because strict white noise is unpredictable, *a fortiori*, expectations and higher moments are unpredictable.

- A *martingale difference sequence* is a sequence of zero-mean, uncorrelated variables such that their conditional expectations given the past values of the series is always zero. Because both expectations and conditional expectations are zero, in a martingale difference sequence, expectations are unpredictable but higher moments, if they exist, may be predictable.

- *White noise* is a sequence of zero-mean, finite variance uncorrelated variables. Because the variables are uncorrelated, in white noise, expectations are linearly unpredictable but may be predicted as nonlinear functions of the past. For example, they may be predictable with a neural network. Higher moments, if they exist, may be predictable.

If the variables are normally distributed, it can be proven that the three concepts coincide. In fact, two uncorrelated normal variables are also independent.

Consider a sequence of zero-mean variables and consider the sequence formed with their sums, so that nth term of the new sequence is the sum of the first n terms of the first sequence. We define the random walk, martingale, and arithmetic random walk as follows:

- An *arithmetic random walk* is the sum of white-noise terms. The mean of an arithmetic random walk is linearly unpredictable but may be predictable with nonlinear predictors. Higher moments may be predictable.

- A *martingale* is the sum of martingale difference sequence terms. The mean of a martingale is unpredictable (linearly and nonlinearly); that is, the expectation of a martingale coincides with its present value. Higher moments may be predictable.

- A *strict random walk* is the sum of strict white-noise terms. A strict random walk is unpredictable: Its mean, variance, and higher moments are all unpredictable.

We summarize the above properties in **Exhibit 1.1** and **Exhibit 1.2**. Exhibit 1.1 summarizes the properties of noise and martingale difference sequences. Exhibit 1.2 summarizes the properties of random walks and martingales.

Exhibit 1.1. Summary of Properties of Noise and Martingale Difference Sequences

Concept	Variables	Predictability
Strict white noise	Zero-mean, finite-variance, IID variables	Expectations and higher moments unpredictable.
Martingale difference sequence	Zero-mean variables such that their conditional expectations are zero	Expectations unpredictable. Higher moments might be predictable.
White noise	Zero-mean, finite-variance uncorrelated variables	Expectations linearly unpredictable. Expectations might be nonlinearly predictable, and higher moments might be predictable.

Exhibit 1.2. Summary of Properties of Random Walks and Martingales

Concept	Increments	Predictability
Strict random walk	Increments are zero-mean, finite-variance, IID variables	Expectations and higher moments are unpredictable.
Martingale	Increments are a martingale difference sequence	Expectations are unpredictable. Higher moments might be predictable.
Random walk	Increments are zero-mean, finite-variance uncorrelated variables	Expectations linearly unpredictable. Expectations might be nonlinearly predictable and higher moments might be predictable

Finally, we have to distinguish between error terms and innovations. It is easy to confuse the two concepts because models can be written in the same way regardless of whether or not error terms are innovations. For example, a random walk and a strict random walk have the same form, but only in the strict random walk are errors innovations.

Any process can be considered formed by two parts: what can be predicted from the past of the process and what cannot be predicted. The part that cannot be predicted is called the *innovation process*. Innovation is not specifically related to a model; it is a characteristic of the process. Innovations are, therefore, unpredictable processes.

Now, consider a model that is supposed to explain empirical data. At every time step, the difference between the model and the empirical data is called the *error* of the model. It is not necessarily true that errors are innovations; that is, it is not necessarily true that errors are unpredictable. If errors are innovations, then the model offers the best possible explanation of data; if not, errors contain residual forecastability. The previous discussion is relevant because it makes a difference whether errors are strict white noise, martingale difference sequences, or simply white noise.

In particular, a random walk whose increments are nonnormal white noise contains a residual structure not explained by the model both at the level of expectations and higher moments. If data follow a martingale model, then expectations are completely explained by the model but higher moments are not.

Why are these apparently arcane considerations practically important? The properties of models depend on the assumptions made about noise. For example, a linear model (see Chapter 7) makes linear predictions of expectations and cannot capture nonlinear events, such as the clustering of volatility. It is thus natural to assume that errors are white noise. In other models, however, different assumptions about noise need to be made; otherwise, the properties of the model conflict with the properties of the noise term.

Now, these considerations have important practical consequences when testing residuals. When testing a model, one has to make sure that the residuals have the properties that we assume they have. Thus, if we use a linear model—say, a linear regression—we will have to make sure that residuals are white noise (that is, that they are uncorrelated). In general, it will suffice to add lags to the set of regressors to remove autocorrelations of residuals.[7] However, if we have to check that residuals are martingale difference sequences or strict white noise, we will have to use more powerful tests. In addition, adding lags will not be sufficient to remove undesired

---

[7]Statements such as this are intended as exemplifications but do not strictly embody sound econometric procedures. Adding lags has side effects, such as making estimations noisier, and cannot be used indiscriminately.

properties of residuals. Models will have to be redesigned. These effects are not marginal; they can have a significant impact on the profitability of a strategy.

Closer Look at Pricing Models. Let's now go back to pricing models. The first hypothesis on equity price processes that was advanced as a solution to the problem of forecastability was the *random walk hypothesis*.[8] Recall from Exhibit 1.1 that the strongest formulation assumes that returns are a sequence of IID variables—that is, a strict random walk.[9] When variables are IID, "independence" means that distributions remain the same regardless of the history of past returns. Therefore, investors are not able to predict future returns by using historical returns. "Identically distributed" means that all returns have the same distribution in every time period. The two conditions entail that, over time, the mean and the variance do not change from period to period (i.e., we are dealing with a *stationary* time-series process). If returns are IID variables, the logarithms of prices follow a random walk and the prices themselves follow a geometric random walk. The IID model is clearly a model without forecastability because the distribution of future returns does not depend on any information set known at the present moment. It does, however, allow stock prices to have a *fixed drift*.

Note from Exhibit 1.1 that there is a weaker form of the random walk hypothesis that requires only that returns at any two different times be uncorrelated. According to this weaker definition, returns are a sequence formed by a constant drift plus white noise. If returns are white noise, however, they are not unpredictable. In fact, white noise, although uncorrelated at every lag, might be predictable in the sense that its expectation might depend on the present information set.

It was initially believed that if one admits that market agents make perfect forecasts, the strict random walk model is the only possible model. However, this conclusion was later proven wrong; the class of admissible models is actually much broader. LeRoy (1973) demonstrated that the strict random walk model is too restricted to be the only possible model and proposed the martingale model—that is, the "fair game" model.

The idea of a martingale is as old as gambling. Actually, the term "martingale" originally indicated a gambling strategy in which the gambler keeps on doubling her bets. In modern statistics, a martingale embodies the idea of a fair game—that is, a game in which at every bet, the gambler has exactly the same probability of winning or losing. In fact, as described in Exhibit 1.2, the martingale is a process in which the expected value of the process at any future date is the actual value of the process.

---

[8]For an explanation of the random walk model, see Chapter 10 in DeFusco, McLeavey, Pinto, and Runkle (2004).

[9]Returns are typically mutually correlated. This correlation does not allow any forecastability, however, because it is a relationship between returns at a given time *t*.

If a price process or a game is represented by a martingale, then the expectation of gains or losses is zero. Note that a random walk with uncorrelated increments is not necessarily a martingale because its expectations are only linearly unpredictable.

Technically, the martingale model applies to the logarithms of prices. Returns are (approximately) the differences of the logarithms of prices. The martingale model requires that the expected value of returns be not predictable, because it is zero or a fixed constant. However, there can be subtle patterns of forecastability for higher moments of the return distribution. Higher moments are those moments of a probability distribution beyond the expected value and variance—for example, skewness and kurtosis.[10] In other words, *the distribution of returns can depend on the present information set provided that the expected value of the distribution remains constant.*

The martingale model does not fully take into consideration risk premiums because it allows higher moments of returns to vary while expected values remain constant. It cannot be a general solution to the problem of what processes are compatible with the assumptions that investors can make perfect probabilistic forecasts.

The definitive answer is ascribable to Harrison and Kreps (1979) and Harrison and Pliska (1981, 1985). They demonstrated that stock prices must indeed be martingales but *after* multiplication for a factor that takes risk into account. Their methodology is mathematically complicated and exceeds the scope of this monograph. The conclusion of their work, however, is that a broad variety of predictable processes are compatible with the assumption that the market is populated by agents capable of making perfect forecasts. Predictability is to the result of the interplay of risk and return.

However, precisely because the market is populated by agents capable of making perfect forecasts, it is not necessarily true that successful predictions will lead to excess returns. For example, it is generally accepted that predicting volatility is easier than predicting returns. The usual explanation of this fact is that investors and asset managers are more interested in returns than in volatility. With the maturing of asset management methods and with increased emphasis on risk–return trade-offs, risk and returns have become equally important. However, this does not imply that both risk and returns have become unpredictable. It is now admitted that predicting combinations of the two is possible.

---

[10]In describing a probability distribution function, it is common to summarize it by using various measures. The four most commonly used measures are location, dispersion, asymmetry, and concentration in tails. In the parlance of the statistician, the four measures are called "statistical moments" or simply "moments." The mean is the first moment and is also referred to as the expected value. The variance is the second moment, skewness is a rescaled third moment, and kurtosis is a rescaled fourth moment.

Is Forecasting Markets Worth the Effort?

What are the implications of this discussion for portfolio managers? Portfolio managers and chief investment officers must decide whether there is potentially sufficient benefit in trying to extract additional information (and thus additional profit) from markets through quantitative research and modeling. A first important conclusion from the discussion is the following:

> It is not true that progress in our ability to forecast will necessarily lead to a simplification in price and return processes. Even if investors were to become perfect forecasters, price and return processes might still exhibit complex patterns of forecastability in both expected values and higher moments, insofar as they might be martingales after dynamically adjusting for risk. No simple conclusion can be reached simply by assuming that investors are perfect forecasters: in fact, it is not true that the ability to forecast prices implies that prices are unpredictable random walks.

When the random walk hypothesis was first advanced, it was believed that forecasting efforts were futile because prices were random walks. However, it seems reasonable to conclude that price processes will always be structured processes simply because investors are trying to forecast them. Modeling and sophisticated forecasting techniques will be needed to understand the risk–return trade-offs offered by the market.

A second point is that the idealized behavior of perfect forecasters does not have much to do with the actual behavior of real-world investors. Real-world investors use relatively simple forecasting techniques, such as linear regressions. When they use judgment, it is fair to say that the possibility of making mistakes is high. The preoccupation with the idealized behavior of markets populated by perfect forecasters seems to be ill placed. The usual defense of the assumption that real investors are perfect forecasters is that it is unreasonable to assume that investors make systematic mistakes. It is claimed that, on average, investors make correct forecasts.

But this is obviously false. Investors can make systematic mistakes and then hit some boundary with painful consequences. The technology/media/telecommunications bubble of the late 1990s is an example. The preoccupation to stay within the strict doctrine of market efficiency has no strong justification. As a matter of fact, field research conducted by The Intertek Group has shown that asset managers are not preoccupied with theoretical considerations of market efficiency. A pragmatic attitude prevails. Markets are considered to be difficult to predict but to exhibit rather complex structures that can be (and indeed are) predicted, either qualitatively or quantitatively.

A third important, and not surprising, consideration is that predictability is not the only path to profitability. If prices behaved as simple models, such as the random walk or the martingale, they could nevertheless exhibit high levels of persistent profitability.[11] The reason is that these models are characterized by a fixed structure of expected returns. Actually, it is the time invariance of expected returns, coupled with the existence of risk premiums, that makes these models unsuitable as long-term models. As we will discuss in Chapter 8, a model like the geometric random walk model of prices leads to exponentially diverging expected returns. This is unrealistic in the long run, because it would lead to the concentration of all market capitalization in one asset. As a consequence, models like the random walk model can only be *approximate* models over *limited* periods of time. This fact, in turn, calls attention to robust estimation methods. A random walk model is not an idealization that represents the final benchmark model: It is only a short-term approximation of what a model able to capture the dynamic feedbacks present in financial markets should be.

Conclusion

Consider our earlier questions: Is it worth attempting to forecast markets with quantitative methods? Is it true that, although the random walk model cannot be theoretically justified, it is the most robust approximation to market behavior we have?

The behavior of markets is the result of not perfectly rational agents but real agents who have limited intelligence, have limited resources, and are subject to unpredictable exogenous events. The action of these agents is in itself a source of uncertainty. As a result, there is no theoretical reason to maintain that the multi-variate random walk is the most robust model. Determining whether the random walk is, indeed, the benchmark model of price processes is an empirical question and has to be addressed empirically. However, it seems clear that markets offer patterns of predictability in returns, volatility, and possibly, higher moments. These patterns might offer opportunities for realizing excess returns; ignoring the patterns will lead to lost opportunities or simply losses. In other words, simple random walk models with risk premiums are not necessarily the safest models. The joint assumption that markets are unforecastable and that there are risk premiums is not necessarily the safest assumption.

---

[11]Perhaps we should explain what we mean by *profitability*. In finance theory, any profit in excess of the riskless profit must be considered risky. Profitability thus entails a risk–return trade-off that an investor judges favorable given his or her risk–return preferences. In the absence of arbitrage, price processes can be transformed into martingales. However, this does not imply that all risk–return trade-offs are equivalent; investors have different risk–return preferences. Positive alphas do not imply arbitrage.

2. General Equilibrium Theories: Concepts and Applicability

Our focus in this chapter is on describing the basic principles underlying general equilibrium theories. We approach the theories not from a theoretical point of view, but from an informal and intuitive standpoint. The intent is to help readers understand the capital asset pricing model and its limitations. The CAPM is probably the best-known general equilibrium theory in finance.

General equilibrium theories can be considered the pinnacle of economic theory. The theories have the status and the mathematical complexity that classical dynamics have in physics. The practical applicability of general equilibrium theories is limited, however, unless drastic approximations are accepted. In addition, there appears to be a good deal of conceptual confusion about the empirical meaning of these theories.

Understanding how general equilibrium theories work requires an understanding of how the decision-making process of agents in the market can be formalized through utility functions. We address this question in this chapter. First, however, we discuss the concept of general equilibrium.[12]

General Equilibrium

Succinctly, the concept of general equilibrium is the following.[13] Markets must always be in "physical equilibrium," in the sense that any transaction requires a seller and a buyer. Supply and demand may be in disequilibrium, however, because the quantity of each good offered for sale at a given market price may not be the same as the quantity that market participants are willing to buy at that price; in such a circumstance, a shortage or glut of the good occurs. The key point is that in a given economy, both supply and demand are functions of one factor: price. General market equilibrium means that in a well-functioning competitive market, prices will immediately adjust so that "supply equals demand" (more precisely, the quantity supplied at the current market price equals the quantity demanded at that price).

---

[12]Bernstein (1992) gives a historical account of the development of modern finance theory and its impact on financial markets. His personal experiences and extensive interviewing of key protagonists result in a lively account.

[13]The classic reference on the subject is Varian (1992).

The existence of market equilibrium is intuitive. Even in daily life we have the experience that if a product is in short supply, prices rise until demand fades and if there is excess supply, prices fall until new buyers are attracted.[14] The rigorous demonstration of the existence of equilibrium, however, hinges on one of the most profound results of modern mathematics—namely, Brouwer's fixed-point theorem.[15]

Market equilibrium as discussed so far is a static, deterministic concept. That is, in this simple setting, demand does not change with time and there is no uncertainty. Arrow and Debreu (1954) extended this concept to an *uncertain* environment in which market participants decide at a given time on the basis of uncertain future prices. Uncertainty is represented by the idea that the economy can be in a multitude of *states*, where each state is associated with a different price. The concept of "state" in this approach is an abstraction. A state is the ensemble of all variables that characterize an economy at a given moment. Different states differ by at least one variable. Because in practice people know only a limited number of variables, researchers have introduced the concept of an abstract state.

The extension of general supply-and-demand theory to an uncertain environment proposed by Arrow and Debreu involves regarding a good in each state as a separate good (so-called state goods or state prices). With this approach, one can take the concepts used in the deterministic case and use them in the uncertain environment. One still needs to know the demand for each good in each state, but conceptually, Arrow and Debreu made a major step forward. Their approach allowed the tools of probability theory to be integrated in a natural way with the mechanics of competitive markets.

At this point, we need to explain how the preferences of market participants can be formalized. This is achieved by introducing the concept of utility functions.

Utility Functions

The concept of utility functions was introduced in economics by the Italian engineer and economist Vilfredo Pareto at the end of the 19th century. A slightly different concept of utility that is used today was introduced by Von Neumann and Morgenstern (1944).

The problem that Pareto and, later, Von Neumann and Morgenstern wanted to solve was how to represent mathematically the decision-making process of market participants—that is, how market participants choose between different

---

[14]This example focuses on changes in demand caused by changes in price, but a focus on changes in supply caused by changes in price is equally instructive.

[15]Brouwer's fixed-point theorem states that if a continuous function maps an interval onto itself, there must be a point where the function has the same value as that of its argument. Geometrically, if a continuous line joins two opposing vertices of a square, there must be a point where the line meets the diagonal.

goods or investment products. A mathematical representation of agents' choices is necessary if the entire market process is to be represented mathematically.

In the 19th century, the principal mathematical tool used in physics and engineering was calculus (today, a broader range of mathematics is used). Therefore, when Pareto introduced a quantitative notion of decision making, he used calculus to represent agents' choices. Agents order their choices of goods (including investment products) quantitatively by associating with each possible decision a value, the decision's so-called utility. According to Pareto, decision making is carried out by computing the utility of each good or service and then selecting the one with the highest utility.[16]

Von Neumann and Morgenstern provided a rigorous logical basis to this reasoning. They assumed that economic agents—investors, for example—are always able to express preferences, in the sense that if they are given two alternatives, they can always determine either that they prefer one to the other or that they are precisely indifferent between the two. In the context of investing, an investor's attitude toward risk—that is, the rate at which the investor is willing to accept an additional unit of risk to earn an additional unit of expected return (the rate that is called the investor's "risk preference")—determines how much risk that investor will take. In the context of Markowitz's mean–variance optimization (see Chapter 3), it determines at what point on the efficient frontier the investor's investment portfolio will lie.

Utility theory assumes that preferences abide by a number of consistency rules. For example, if choice A is preferred over choice B and choice B is preferred over choice C, then choice A must be preferred over choice C. Under these assumptions, it can be mathematically demonstrated that one can assign a number, the utility, to each possible choice. A *utility function* is a function that assigns a utility number to every possible choice. Utility theory further assumes that all decision makers try to maximize their utility

Without going deeply into a mathematical characterization of utility functions, we can summarize by saying that many different utility functions—that is, different functional forms in the mathematical sense—have been proposed to describe various aspects of agents' decision-making processes. For example, an important issue is whether agents can be satiated so that their utility functions become zero for certain choices (in other words, so that the acquisition of an additional unit of a good produces no additional satisfaction). The answer is certainly yes for such goods as perishable food, but for most goods, the answer to the question is unclear.

Utility is an abstract concept: Agents do not explicitly maximize their utility when making decisions. For the purpose of modeling, however, agents can be assumed to

---

[16]In its original form, Pareto's law states that there is a linear relationship between the logarithms of income, I, and the number of people that earn more than I. A broad range of phenomena, such as the populations of cities within a country, follow the Pareto law, which is also known as the Zipf law or Zipf distribution.

do just that. Utility theory further assumes that the system by which an individual maps choices into quantities of utility is fixed and predetermined at any given point in time, although it may change deterministically over time. The theory of utility functions is in contrast to our everyday perception of human behavior as unpredictable; it embodies the belief that human behavior is perfectly predictable (i.e., deterministic), albeit within the restricted domain of economic decision making.[17]

The representation of decision-making processes as the maximization of utility has been criticized on various grounds. One of the criticisms is that decision making is not as deterministic as utility functions assume it to be. For example, humans are subject to peer pressure and fads and are, in general, influenced by others. Canetti's *Crowds and Power* gives a chilling description of how behavior changes depending on whether people are acting as individuals or in groups.[18]

The rationality of decision making has been much discussed in the context of the psychology of financial decision making. *Behavioral finance*, a more recent addition to financial theory, applies psychological considerations to understand how investors' decision-making processes are affected by emotions and cognitive errors.[19] For example, behavioral finance studies whether (and how) investors overreact or underreact to the arrival of new information and news. The study of psychology and other social sciences can provide considerable insight into the efficiency of financial markets and may provide explanations of market anomalies and nonrational investor behavior.

Finally, the theory of *mutually interacting agents* applied to economics explicitly recognizes that there are pairwise influences between agents: What one person does may depend directly on what someone else does. Pairwise influences run contrary to the representation of decision making with static utility functions. In fact, static utility functions assume that there is only one central signal—the price—on which all decisions are based; in this framework, each decision maker makes his or her decision alone without reference to what other people decide. The classical utility maximization paradigm excludes the direct exchange of information and mutual influence between agents. The utility maximization paradigm can be adapted to a framework of mutually interacting agents, however, by making utility functions depend on mutual interactions.

---

[17]The question as to whether the predictability of human decision making contradicts the concept of free will was the subject of philosophical and moral debate for centuries. Economists were able to avoid the problem by making the argument that economic decision making is technically rational and does not involve any moral considerations. Although the rationality of agents' economic decisions has been questioned, the moral dimension of economic decision making is rarely discussed.

[18]Canetti (1984). This book was first published in German in 1960 as *Masse und Macht* by Claassen Verlag, Hamburg, Germany. The English translation, *Crowds and Power*, was published in 1962. Canetti was awarded the Nobel Prize in Literature 1981.

[19]For an overview of behavioral finance, see Barberis and Thaler (2003).

Utility and Uncertainty

The concept of utility discussed so far assumes perfect knowledge (i.e., the absence of uncertainty) about choices. We will now introduce uncertainty and show how utility functions can embody a risk–return trade-off. Note that we will deal with uncertainty about the future *consequences* of choices (for example, the returns on an investment), not uncertainty about the way the choice is made; that is, the utility function itself is not uncertain.

To understand how to combine utility and probability, consider the problem of determining the composition of a portfolio formed by only one risk-free asset and one risky asset—say, a stock. As already observed, uncertainty is represented by the fact that the economy can be in a number of states. Thus, at any future date, a multitude of different prices for the risky asset is possible. Given only one risky asset, each economic state is identified by one price and thus by one return (the price and return of the risk-free asset are the same in all states).

Investors must determine the proportion of their funds to allocate to each of the two assets. A price and a return are associated with each state, so based on the proportions or weights of the assets, the portfolio return can be determined in each state. The utility function is then defined so that each return carries an associated utility level; this utility function then indicates the utility of each possible return on the investment. If a probability number is associated with each state, one can compute the (statistically) expected value of the utility. If the portfolio has a high proportion of the risky asset, its returns will exhibit a lot of fluctuation, with some states having a high level of utility and other states having a low level of utility. According to utility theory, an investor will choose those weights that correspond to the highest expected utility.

In this formulation, the risk–return trade-off is implemented in the way utility is associated with returns. For example, if high returns have a high utility, they will have a considerable weight in the optimization process, even if their probability of occurring is low. Different utility functions (i.e., different ways to associate utility with returns) generate different trade-offs.

There is another way to generate a risk–return trade-off with utility functions. If one knows the distribution of returns, one can define a utility that is a function of both returns and the variance of returns. Each portfolio has a specific expected return and variance. The utility function is defined as a function of portfolio return and variance. Given the distribution of returns, one can compute the distribution of utility and its expectation. Portfolios can be chosen by maximizing utility defined as a function of expected returns and variances.

General Equilibrium and the Utility Function

Now, we will take another look at general equilibrium in light of the utility function. We will use the CAPM as the setting. In this setting, we have a number of risky assets and one risk-free asset. There are also a number of investors, who own all the available assets. Because we will consider only one period, each investor's utility is defined as a function of the returns of his or her portfolio at the end of the period. Each investor knows the joint probability of returns at the end of the period—that is, the probability of returns taken all together—and will choose weights that maximize the expected return of his or her portfolio.

In equilibrium (and this condition is the essence of general equilibrium), the distribution of returns will be such that all investors will reach the optimum of their utility functions and there will be no trading. This general equilibrium condition places restrictions on return expectations. Assuming normal distributions of returns and utility functions equivalent to mean–variance optimization, the classic CAPM embodies these restrictions by saying that the excess return of each stock over the riskless rate is proportional to the market's excess return over the risk-free rate (the proportion being the beta of the stock). Generally, all investors' utility functions can be grouped together so that their collective action is equivalent to that of the so-called *representative agent*.

In a multiperiod setting, we can consider trade-offs that are not possible in the single-period setting. In a single-period setting, agents optimize the expected utility of returns at the end of the period, which is equivalent to optimizing the utility of expected wealth at the end of the period. In a multiperiod setting, agents optimize the utility of a stream of consumption and final wealth is considered the final consumption. If no intermediate consumption occurs, the multiperiod setting is equivalent to a single-period setting unless one imposes a utility function defined on intermediate wealth rather than on a consumption stream. But an investor may be concerned with the fluctuations of his or her wealth, which requires considering utility functions at different time points. Thus, we need to determine how the utility function varies as a function of time. Although various modeling options exist, the end result of all of them is that the investors' utilities are functions of time.

Although a discussion of general equilibrium in a multiperiod setting is highly technical and beyond the scope of this monograph, the principle of general equilibrium is the same in a multiperiod setting as in a single-period setting. The key ingredients of the general equilibrium theory are as follows:
* a set of price processes for all the assets involved,
* a set of investors and their relative utility functions, and
* optimization of agent utility.

In the general equilibrium framework, investors know the price process. Thus, they base their decisions on the price processes the assets follow—such as a random walk. Agents optimize their portfolios on the basis of their forecasts. The result of this optimization process creates demand and supply as each agent rebalances his or her portfolio. In equilibrium, the prices resulting from demand and supply do not produce any effect on the returns used by agents in their decision process. In other words, conceptually, there is no *feedback* from prices to returns.

General equilibrium theories are theoretical constructs in which unobservable utility functions are an integral (and abstract) part of the theory. In other words, these theories must be viewed as rather complex analytical descriptions of the real world. Testing general equilibrium theories, therefore, has required that researchers consider the context. For example, if a general equilibrium theory is specified with utility functions and all the exogenous processes, researchers can generally find a number of testable conclusions. Perhaps the most well known is the CAPM conclusion that the market portfolio must be mean–variance efficient.

In summary, general equilibrium theories provide an idealized framework for modeling and understanding individuals' choices and the evolution of prices.

Agents and General Equilibrium

From the preceding discussion, readers should realize that the "agents" who appear in a general equilibrium formulation of a model have little to do with the economic agents one might encounter in real life. Utility-optimizing agents, if not purely mathematical fictions, have to be considered an idealization. The question is whether the idealization is close enough to reality to be useful.

In a famous essay, Friedman (1953) introduced the idea that economic theory is not intended to describe reality; it should be evaluated on whether it explains empirically ascertainable phenomena. He wrote:

> The relevant question to ask about the "assumptions" of a theory is not whether they are descriptively "realistic," for they never are, but whether they are sufficiently good approximations for the purpose in hand. And this question can be answered only by seeing whether the theory works, which means if it yields sufficiently accurate predictions. (p. 15)

In this connection, a long debate has opposed two views of financial agents. One view holds that financial agents are "infinitely rational" agents who know the true stochastic process of the economy. The other, more recent, view holds that they are "boundedly rational agents"; they are closer to real agents than are infinitely rational agents because they form forecasts and expectations based on limited information, have limited ability to interpret that information, and thus make mistakes.

This debate is fairly academic; agents are obviously boundedly rational. Any real person claiming to be an infinitely rational agent would be laughed at. As demonstrated by Harrison and Kreps (1979), however, any price system generated by a system of boundedly rational agents, provided the system does not admit arbitrage opportunities, can also be described by a model that assumes infinitely rational agents. Ultimately, the objective is to arrive at a reasonably approximate description of financial price processes. Therefore, the description of financial price processes as the result of the optimizing behavior of rational agents is a useful framework.

Despite the usefulness of such frameworks, users should be aware of their limitations. For example, the classic framework of single-period optimization proved to be very useful in bringing discipline to the investment process. In particular, single-period optimization brought to asset management the following key elements: (1) consideration of the risk–return trade-off and (2) consideration of correlations. In practice, however, agents apply other considerations. First and foremost, agents consider the uncertainty of the forecasting process. For an agent who is a less-than-perfect forecaster of returns, variances, and correlations, optimization is risky because it can magnify forecasting errors.

Understandably, then, the profession is experiencing a growing interest in portfolio construction techniques that are more robust (that is, less sensitive to forecast error) than classical mean–variance optimization based on utility maximization. Research conducted by The Intertek Group for this monograph, the findings of which are summarized in Chapter 11, revealed that a significant fraction of the surveyed firms are using or are experimenting with forecasting techniques. At the same time, the research has revealed a growing uneasiness with the usability of these new tools. The more pragmatic approach, influenced by this notion of "robustness," is prevailing.

In principle, the conceptual tools for analyzing markets populated with non-rational or boundedly rational agents exist. The camps of practitioners and researchers in this new field, however, are presently far apart. On the one hand, many practitioners would benefit from a clear understanding of the theory behind boundedly rational interacting agents and behavioral finance. On the other hand, researchers in this field would benefit from a clear understanding of the practical needs of the investment management community. A convergence of theory and practice would benefit the whole financial community.

3. Extended Framework for Applying Modern Portfolio Theory

In discussing the application to modern portfolio theory of robust estimation and optimization methods, we first briefly review the methodology of mean–variance optimization and then discuss how robust methods overcome some of the common pitfalls associated with this framework. In particular, we discuss issues related to forecasting returns, diversification, estimation of the covariance matrix, and optimization.

The Mean–Variance Framework Reviewed

In 1952, Harry M. Markowitz addressed a fundamental question in financial decision making: How should an investor allocate his or her funds among the possible investment choices?[20] Prior to Markowitz, this question had received two different responses. One was the response of the speculator, according to which an investor—using judgment and intuition to understand how John Maynard Keynes' (1935) "animal spirits" dominated financial markets[21]—should invest in those assets that he or she believes offer the best prospect for returns. The other was the response of the financial analyst and was centered on the notion of value: Fundamental analysis can discover the true value of an asset, and the investor should invest in those assets that offer the highest value given the price at which the asset is trading.

In Markowitz's 1952 paper, which became one of the most influential works in finance theory, he introduced a critical innovation. He suggested that investors

---

[20]For a review of this framework, see Chapter 11 in DeFusco, McLeavey, Pinto, and Runkle (2004).
[21]In Keynes' economic thinking, psychological elements play a fundamental role. Keynes argued that inexplicable changes in spontaneous confidence can be responsible for economic fluctuations. "Animal spirits" is the term he coined to express the state of spontaneous confidence. In *The General Theory of Employment, Interest and Money*, he wrote, "Even apart from the instability due to speculation, there is the instability due to the characteristic of human nature that a large proportion of our positive activities depend on spontaneous optimism rather than mathematical expectations, whether moral or hedonistic or economic. Most, probably, of our decisions to do something positive, the full consequences of which will be drawn out over many days to come, can only be taken as the result of animal spirits—a spontaneous urge to action rather than inaction, and not as the outcome of a weighted average of quantitative benefits multiplied by quantitative probabilities" (pp. 161–162).

should consider risk as well as return specifically, they should decide the allocation of their investments on the basis of a trade-off between risk and return.[22] The idea that sound financial decision making is a quantitative trade-off between risk and return was revolutionary for two reasons. First, it posited that one could make a quantitative evaluation of risk and return *jointly* by considering all investments and their *correlations* (i.e., their joint movements). Second, it posited that one could optimize even large portfolios.

In making the critical assumption that determining the joint probability distribution of returns of all possible investments is possible, Markowitz introduced to investment management the notion of a quantitative evaluation of risk and returns. A key aspect of Markowitz's risk–return framework, known as "mean–variance optimization" and considered the cornerstone of modern portfolio theory (MPT), is the consideration of correlations.[23] This concept was foreign to classical financial analysis, which revolved around the notion of the value of single investments.

The Markowitz framework is a one-period framework. Investors decide the allocation of investments at time t with estimates of returns (or, equivalently, their wealth) at some future date $t + \Delta t$.[24] Markowitz assumed that investment returns can be represented by a joint normal distribution.[25] The bulk of the distribution lies around the center (mean), and the "tails" of the distribution—that is, the regions far from the center—are very thin. Thus, in a normal distribution, the probability of extreme events is negligible.

The normal distribution is perhaps the most fundamental distribution in probability theory. Although it was introduced by Abraham de Moivre (1667–1754), the normal distribution is generally associated with the German mathematician Karl Gauss (1777–1855); in fact, the normal distribution is also known as the Gaussian distribution. Its popularity rests on a fundamental result proven by Gauss, the *central limit theorem*, according to which the distribution of the sum of a large number of

---

[22]Markowitz was awarded the Nobel Prize in Economic Sciences in 1990 for this work.

[23]Markowitz also understood early in the development of computers the potential they offered in estimating moments (e.g., mean and variance, skewness, and kurtosis) and correlations and to optimize.

[24]An investment strategy that considers only one period ahead is called a "myopic strategy"; an investment strategy that jointly considers multiple periods ahead is called a "far-sighted strategy."

[25]In his 1952 paper, Markowitz did not explicitly mention normal distributions. But because his analysis considered only the first two moments, mean and variance, we can say that Markowitz implicitly assumed that return distributions are normal, in the sense that any nonnormal behavior is considered irrelevant. (Given the first two moments, it can be formally demonstrated that the normal distribution as defined by those two moments is the only distribution that does not introduce spurious information; that is, assuming any distribution other than normal would spuriously introduce information not based on the available data.) We use the assumption of normal distribution of returns here because we believe it helps in understanding the mean–variance principle.

independent random variables is approximately normal, even if the variables themselves have nonnormal distributions, as long as their variances are finite.[26]

In view of this result, Markowitz's assumption was reasonable because investment returns can be considered the sum of many independent events. This assumption is still the basis of much of today's financial econometrics, but it is being questioned (we will come back to this controversy later in the chapter).

The assumption that returns are jointly normal allows a fundamental simplification of the model describing them. A jointly normal distribution of returns on multiple assets is perfectly described by (1) an array of expected returns and (2) a variance–covariance matrix. The variance–covariance matrix is the matrix in which the entry at the crossing of the ith row and the jth column is the covariance between asset i and asset j. The diagonal entries are the variances. Under the assumption of the joint normal distribution of returns and given the expected returns of each asset and their variance–covariance matrix, the expected return and the variance of any portfolio can be derived from the portfolio weights by using simple algebra.

Markowitz's mean–variance principle posits that the risk associated with a portfolio expected return is measured by the portfolio's variance. Consider an investor's return objective. If the desired return is feasible, then an infinite number of portfolios achieve the return objective. Among these portfolios, the problem for the investor is to choose the portfolio that has the minimum variance; all other portfolios are considered to be "inefficient." This problem is a *minimization* (or *optimization*) problem whose solution can be obtained through one of the many optimizers now freely or commercially available. Markowitz's mean–variance principle can be stated alternatively by prescribing that, for any desired variance, investors choose the portfolio that offers the maximum return.

We can sum up Markowitz's mean–variance optimization theory as follows:[27]

- End-of-period returns are jointly normally distributed.
- All an investor needs to know are the expected returns of each asset and their variance–covariance matrix.
- The expected value (i.e., the mean) and the variance of the return of any portfolio can be determined as algebraic expressions of the weights of the assets in the portfolio.
- For any desired return, investors should choose the portfolio that has the lowest variance.
- The portfolio choice is a minimization problem that can be solved with optimization software packages.[28]

---

[26]There are distributions with infinite variance. Samples extracted from these distributions exhibit a variance that grows with the size of sample.

[27]In economics, a distinction is made between *positive* theories that describe the economic state of affairs and *normative* theories that prescribe a given behavior. Markowitz's theory is considered a normative theory because it prescribes investors' behavior.

[28]For practical considerations in selecting optimization software, see Chapter 9.

The mean–variance optimization principle does not identify a single best ("optimal") portfolio. It only identifies the best for a given desired return or desired variance. The mean–variance principle identifies the set of all optimal variance-return pairs, called the "Markowitz efficient frontier." Investors are advised to choose portfolios that are on this frontier. The smallest variance that can be achieved in a portfolio of risky assets has a lower bound; the resulting portfolio is the "global minimum variance" portfolio. Furthermore, if the amount of leverage that can be used is constrained, then the maximum obtainable expected return of all the portfolios on the efficient frontier has an upper bound. This portfolio, often referred to as the "maximum return" portfolio, will, of course, be the riskiest portfolio—the one with the highest volatility—of all the portfolios on the efficient frontier. It will also contain just one asset, the highest-expected-return (and riskiest) asset.

Diversification. The purpose of diversification is to reduce volatility in the portfolio. An investor can achieve diversification by adding assets to the portfolio and, in particular, adding assets that have low correlations with one another.

To understand the process of variance reduction, consider the following three cases. (Assume that the assets all have the same finite variance.) First, if the asset returns are perfectly correlated—that is, if all correlation coefficients are equal to 1—variance cannot be reduced. The asset returns move together perfectly; therefore, from the point of view of variance reduction, choosing more than one asset provides no benefit. Second, if the asset returns are independent, then the variance of a portfolio of N assets is $1/N$ of the variance of each asset. Being independent, most return fluctuations, by pure chance, will cancel each other. Finally, consider the case of perfect negative correlation. This case is interesting because, although all asset returns can be perfectly correlated, it is not possible for all asset returns to be perfectly negatively correlated. To see this point, consider two asset returns and suppose that they are perfectly negatively correlated; that is, the two returns fluctuate in exactly opposite directions. Now, add a third asset. Clearly, it cannot be perfectly negatively correlated with both.

Suppose the set of assets from which investors may choose a portfolio is small—say, the pool is 10 assets. In general, if the set is broadened—say, from 10 to 20—the investor achieves a considerable advantage in terms of variance reduction. If the investor continues to add assets, however, the variance reduction grows progressively smaller until the point at which adding assets provides no practical advantage. A *well-diversified* portfolio is a portfolio whose variance cannot be further reduced by adding assets.[29]

[29]The number of equity assets that are apparently needed to achieve an optimal level of diversification has significantly changed over the years. At the end of the 1960s, Evans and Archer (1968) suggested that as few as 20 stocks should be sufficient to achieve a good level of diversification, but more recent studies (see, for example, Campbell, Lettau, Malkiel, and Xu 2001; Malkiel 2002) have found that as many as 200 stocks are necessary to achieve a good level of diversification today because individual stock variance and correlations have increased over time.

Mean–Variance Utility Optimization. Mean–variance analysis as discussed in the previous sections does not allow an investor to identify a uniquely optimal portfolio. To identify a uniquely optimal portfolio, investors need to specify their risk–return preferences—that is, their mean–variance preferences. In fact, mean–variance analysis identifies *all* mean–variance pairs; the investor must identify his or her *preferred* mean–variance pair.

To solve this problem in a mathematical framework, one needs utility functions, as discussed in Chapter 2. Suppose an investor has defined his or her utility function as a function of mean and variance. That is, the investor is able to associate a utility number to any mean–variance pair. (Note that utility defined in this way is a deterministic function.) The uncertainty associated with the future behavior of portfolios is now entirely represented by this mean–variance pair.

Given a utility function, the portfolio choice problem becomes the problem of maximizing utility. There are two additional important logical elements in the definition of a utility-based framework. First, note that an investor maximizes utility, which we have defined as a function of mean and variance, by determining the weights of the assets in the portfolio. Thus, optimization is about finding the asset mix, or vector of holdings weights, that produces the desired portfolio mean and variance.

The second element is that we must go from variance to the square root of variance, standard deviation. This step is useful for defining such properties as risk aversion. "Expected return" and "variance" are not homogeneous terms because variance is defined as the expected *square* of the fluctuations of returns around their mean. To define risk aversion in simple terms, we need to measure risk and returns in the same units.

Markowitz mean–variance analysis assumes a utility function that is proportional to the expected return minus a weighting factor times the square of standard deviation. The weighting factor is called the "coefficient of risk aversion." A utility function of this type is a quadratic function of the portfolio weights. The corresponding optimization problem is thus a quadratic optimization problem.

Eventually, higher moments could be included. For example, an investor may "like" skewness (denoted S_3) but be averse to kurtosis (denoted S_4), so his utility function is given by

$$U = \mu - k_1\sigma^2 - k_2 S_3 - k_3 S_4,$$

where k_1, k_2, and k_3 are the coefficients of aversion to, respectively, variance, skewness, and kurtosis. Note that k_2 would be negative in this example (thus the product, $k_2 S_3$, is positive) and adds to utility because the investor likes skewness; that is, all other things being equal, he prefers a distribution with positive skewness to one with zero skewness).

Expected Utility Maximization. In the previous section, we defined utility as a deterministic function of expected returns and standard deviation of returns. In other words, we considered only the first two central moments of a probability distribution (expected return and standard deviation) and ignored higher moments of the probability distribution. The utility framework can be generalized, however, to account for any distribution. In this expanded utility framework, we define utility as a function of the entire probability distribution of returns; then, portfolio weights are determined by maximizing the expectation of utility.[30]

Robust Methods of Applying Mean–Variance Optimization

Mean–variance optimization (MVO), although formulated in the early 1950s, was not immediately applied in practice for various reasons. Some of the impediments are related to the ways in which asset management firms were and are structured, and some are related to technical problems. In this section, we discuss a few of the reasons why the application of MVO slowed down.

A significant barrier to the spread of MVO is that adequate computing power at a cost affordable by a medium-sized asset management firm became available only in the 1990s. Before then, the cost of computing and storage was too high for wide deployment of security-level optimization. (Because the number of asset classes is limited, optimization at the asset-class level could be conducted in the late 1970s and early 1980s.) The cost and difficulty of programming was also a significant barrier. The cost of even off-the-shelf applications plus the cost of data were prohibitive for most firms. So, many organizations could not adopt MVO in full.

In addition, the crucial inputs to mean–variance optimization—namely, estimates of expected returns and the variance–covariance matrix—pose key practical challenges in applying MVO. If a portfolio manager feeds an optimizer historical mean returns and the historical variance–covariance matrix, the results obtained will be poor. The reason is that for any realistic number of assets, the empirical mean returns and the variance–covariance matrix are noisy estimates of the true expected returns and the variance–covariance matrix.

For an idea of the severity of the problem created by having to have a large number of estimates, consider estimating the variance–covariance matrix of the S&P 500 Index. Suppose we use two years of data—that is, roughly 500 data points per return series. In total, 500 × 500 = 250,000 data points are available. Although this number seems large, keep in mind that the variance–covariance matrix of the S&P 500 has approximately 125,000 entries. Thus, on average, only two data points

---

[30]Chapter 2 of Fabozzi, Focardi, and Kolm (2006a) offers a discussion of the expected utility framework and describes many classes of utility functions.

per entry are available for estimates. The result is that many entries of the empirical variance–covariance matrix are simply pure noise.

Suppose we feed this covariance matrix into an optimizer. Any optimizer seeks the best combinations of return and variance. Unless we adopt specialized "robust methods" (which we describe in the next section), the optimizer will not be able to distinguish noise—or estimation error—from true information. The optimization software treats all the inputs as deterministic and error free, which puts statistical outliers or simply bad estimates in a position of power in the optimizer. The result is the production of so-called corner portfolios. A corner portfolio is a portfolio with a high concentration in a few stocks that, because of estimation error and pure noise, seem to offer exceptional optimization opportunities. In short, the optimizer is maximizing estimation errors. Many organizations that tried to implement MVO had negative experiences primarily as a result of this phenomenon of error maximization. What was needed was a robust methodology for estimation and optimization.

Robust Estimation. Modeling returns is perhaps the most critical issue in implementing the Markowitz framework.[31] The Markowitz framework per se does not require that returns be a sequence of independently and identically distributed (IID) variables (i.e., that returns be independent from previous returns), only that returns be conditionally normal.[32] The problem in modeling returns is the difficulty of estimating the variance–covariance matrix of the normal distribution of returns A number of approaches to estimating expected returns and the variance–covariance matrix have been tried: the empirical approach, the factor-based approach, the clustering approach, the Bayesian approach, and the stochastic volatility approach.

■ *Empirical approach.* If the portfolio manager adopts a model of returns as a sequence of IID variables, the manager can estimate the expected (future) returns and the variance–covariance matrix by using the empirical (past) means and empirical variance–covariance matrix. In this approach, the expected return is calculated as the historical arithmetic average return. The expected variance–covariance matrix is obtained similarly by assuming "future equals past." Although this estimation is theoretically correct for large IID samples, the results are poor in practice. In fact, historical estimates are noisy, so using the historical means and variance–covariance matrix in portfolio optimization typically produces the corner portfolios. In addition, if the sequence of returns is not IID—for example, if returns are mean reverting, estimation errors will be significant.

---

[31]For further discussion, see Chapter 4 of Fabozzi, Focardi, and Kolm (2006a).
[32]If returns are normal but not independent and exhibit some forecastability, the Markowitz framework can be applied. If returns are not independent, however, use of a one-period-ahead framework is problematic because, in that case, there are forecastable trade-offs between transaction costs and returns. We discuss this aspect later in the chapter.

■ *Factor-based approach.* A key problem in estimating the variance–covariance matrix is the large number of entries in the variance–covariance matrix in comparison with the number of available sample data points. As a result of the small number of data points, covariances are noisy. Very large or very small covariances may appear by chance. The factor-based approach solves the problem by reducing the number of covariances to those between a restricted number of common *factors*. The entire variance–covariance matrix is, therefore, determined by the variance–covariance matrix of the factors. Then, each asset must be characterized as a "portfolio" (or weighted sum) of factor exposures so that the variance–covariance estimates for factors can be applied to holdable assets.

In a factor model, every individual return is represented as a weighted sum of a number of factors plus some noise. In this way, the covariance between any two assets is a weighted average of the covariances between the factors. Factors themselves can be company fundamental factors (e.g., financial ratios) or economic factors (e.g., the unemployment rate) or can be determined through statistical techniques, such as principal-component analysis (see Chapter 9).

■ *Clustering approach.* The clustering approach is based on averaging the entries of the empirical correlation matrix. The correlation matrix is obtained by replacing covariances with correlations. The correlation matrix plus the array (or vector) of individual variances gives the same information as the variance–covariance matrix. Because averaging the entire matrix would be an inefficient solution, machine-learning techniques (see Chapter 6) are used to identify *clusters* (i.e., subsets of assets that are similar). A robust correlation matrix is obtained by averaging over the different clusters.

■ *Bayesian approach.* The Bayesian approach is slightly different from the approach of classical finance . The classical approach to estimating expected returns assumes that the "true" expected returns and covariances of returns are unknown and *fixed*. The portfolio manager obtains a point estimate (i.e., an estimate of the most likely return represented by a single number) by using forecasting models of observed market data and proprietary data. The Bayesian approach, in contrast, assumes that the "true" expected returns are unknown and *random*.

Named after the English mathematician Thomas Bayes (1702–1761), the Bayesian approach is based on a *subjective* interpretation of probability. A probability distribution is used to represent an investor's (or asset manager's) belief about the probability that a specific event will actually occur. This probability distribution, called the "prior distribution," reflects an investor's judgment before any data are observed. When more information is provided, the investor's judgment about the probability of an event occurring may change. Bayes' rule is the formula for computing the probability distribution after more information is obtained. This new probability distribution is called the "posterior distribution."

In Bayesian models, a posterior distribution of expected return is derived by combining the forecast from the empirical data with the prior distribution. For example, in the Black–Litterman model (Black and Litterman 1990, 1992), an estimate of future expected returns is based on combining forecasts based on market equilibrium (e.g., capital asset pricing model equilibrium) with an investor's views. Such views are expressed as absolute or relative deviations from equilibrium together with confidence levels of the views. The confidence levels are measured by the standard deviation of the views.

The Black–Litterman expected return is calculated as a weighted average of the market equilibrium and the investor's views. The weights depend on (1) the volatility of each asset and its correlations with the other assets and (2) the degree of confidence in each forecast. The resulting expected return, which is the mean of the posterior distribution, is then used as an input in the classical mean–variance optimization process. Portfolio weights computed in this fashion tend to be more intuitive and less sensitive than other methods to small changes in the original inputs, such as forecasts of market equilibrium, investor's views, and the covariance matrix. The Black–Litterman model modifies the inputs to the mean–variance framework, but the risk–return optimization is the same as in Markowitz's classical approach.

The attractiveness of the Bayesian approach is that it allows a portfolio manager to incorporate into formal models some exogenous insight, such as the manager's judgment. This insight might well be the most valuable input used in the model. In addition, because portfolio managers may not be willing to give up control to a "black box," the incorporation of exogenous insights into formal models through Bayesian techniques is one way of giving the manager better control in a quantitative framework. Forecasts are represented through probability distributions that can be modified or adjusted to incorporate other sources of information. The only restriction is that such additional information (i.e., the manager's views) be combined with the existing model through the laws of probability. In effect, incorporating Bayesian views into a model allows a manager to "rationalize" subjectivity within a formal quantitative framework. "[T]he rational investor is a Bayesian," Markowitz (1987, p. 57) noted.

■ *Stochastic-volatility approach.* Stochastic-volatility models treat volatility as a variable term to be forecasted. Generally, the entire covariance matrix, not only volatility, can be regarded as a set of variable terms to be forecasted. Estimates of the covariance matrix are not stable, however, but vary over time, so this aspect must be dealt with.

An early (and not entirely satisfactory) attempt to deal with this problem was covariance-matrix discounting, which assumes that the covariance matrix changes over time. At any moment, there is a "local" covariance matrix. The covariance matrix is estimated as a weighted average of past local covariance matrices, and the weighting factors typically decay exponentially over time. Since being introduced in the 1980s, covariance discounting has been used as a component of applied Bayesian forecasting models in financial applications.[33]

However, covariance-matrix discounting does not have any real predictive power; the methods (simplistically) provide exponentially smoothed estimates of the local covariance structure (i.e., the covariance matrix that is supposed to hold at a given moment) within the Bayesian modeling framework. Covariance-matrix discounting *estimates* change; it does not *forecast* change. As a consequence, models based on these methods tend to work reasonably well in environments where volatility changes slowly, but they do poorly in rapidly changing markets or when structural change occurs.

Dynamic factor models (see Chapter 5) that explicitly capture change through patterns of variation in process parameters throughout time provide greater flexibility than does covariance-matrix discounting. In dynamic factor models, the covariance matrix is driven by a multifactor model. This approach has shown significant improvement in the short-term forecasting of multiple financial and economic time series and appears to be a promising technique also for the intermediate and long term. Although dynamic factor models are computationally demanding and often require time-consuming simulations, increasing computer power and recent advances in Markov chain Monte Carlo methods will contribute to growing use of these models.

Robust Portfolio Optimization. As discussed previously, the inputs to the portfolio allocation process are unknown and have to be estimated. Any statistical estimate is subject to error—estimation error. Therefore, it would be useful if the portfolio optimization problem could handle the inputs given as ranges, or even as statistical distributions, rather than as the traditional point estimates. Moreover, MVO assumes that all estimates are equally precise or imprecise and treats all securities equally. But it would be desirable if, when managers calculate optimal portfolios, the differences in precision of the estimates could be explicitly incorporated in the process. Providing this benefit is the underlying aim of robust portfolio optimization.

For simplicity, assume that a portfolio manager knows the correct covariance matrix and that only the expected returns are estimated with some error. Some securities may have larger estimation errors than others, resulting in greater standard errors and also larger confidence intervals around those estimates. Robust portfolio optimization takes these differences in uncertainty into account. In a nutshell, the robust counterpart of mean–variance solutions calculates the portfolio weights that maximize the expected return subject to a certain level of portfolio standard deviation, not by using the estimated expected returns alone, but by using the worst-case

---

[33]Covariance-matrix discounting was introduced in the second half of the 1980s; a recent discussion is provided in Aguilar and West (2000).

realization of the expected return from the range given by the confidence interval. The result is a "max-min" problem: One maximizes the expected return of the portfolio given the most pessimistic realization of the expected returns of the assets. (Please note that this method is not the only possible robust optimization method.)

What is the result of this procedure? Because we are using the worst-case expected return, when our confidence is low for a particular security (i.e., the confidence interval is large), we will decrease the resulting portfolio weight. Conversely, when our confidence is high, we consider the reliability of the estimated expected return to be higher and we set the security's weight in our portfolio much closer to the weight that would be obtained from the classical mean–variance solution.

We chose a simple representation of uncertainty—the estimation risk—in the estimates of the expected returns. But many more generalizations are possible and result in more complicated *uncertainty sets*. For example, we could consider uncertainty in the expected returns and the covariance matrix simultaneously. The basic principle, however, remains the same.

To construct a robust portfolio, a manager needs to understand how uncertainty in return and correlation estimation translates into a distribution of portfolios. Monte Carlo methods offer a "brute force" approach; that is, in these methods, one simulates a large number of different portfolios. This approach is computationally onerous because every portfolio requires a separate optimization. Robust optimization is a more parsimonious approach. Introduced by Ben-Tal and Nemirovski (1998, 1999) and by El Ghaoui and Lebret (1977), robust optimization allows a portfolio manager to solve the robust version of the mean–variance optimization problem efficiently in about the same time as needed for solving the classical mean–variance optimization problem. The technique explicitly uses the distribution from the estimation process to find a robust portfolio in one single optimization. It thereby incorporates uncertainties about inputs into a deterministic framework. The classical portfolio optimization methods—such as mean–variance optimization, using the maximum Sharpe ratio, and using value at risk—all have robust counterparts that can be solved in roughly the same amount of time as the original optimization (see Goldfarb and Iyengar 2003).

Robust mean–variance portfolios are more stable than other portfolios as inputs change and tend to perform better than classical mean–variance portfolios. Moreover, the robust optimization framework offers a lot of flexibility and many interesting new applications. For example, robust portfolio optimization can exploit the existence of *statistically equivalent portfolios* that are cheaper to trade into. This capability is important in large-scale portfolio management involving many complex constraints on transaction costs, turnover, or market impact. For instance, with robust optimization, a manager can calculate the new portfolio that (1) minimizes trading costs with respect to the current holdings and (2) has an expected portfolio return and variance that are statistically equivalent to those of the classical mean–variance portfolio.

Finally, the robust counterparts to the classical mean–variance problem are not quadratic programming problems. The structure of the robust optimization problem depends on the particular uncertainty set used, but most uncertainty sets being used in practice lead to "second-order cone programs," which can be solved by modern optimization algorithms in about the same time as solving the classical mean–variance problem.[34]

Departure from Normality: Portfolio Allocation for General Return Distributions. The classical mean–variance framework relies on the assumption that the return distribution can be characterized by the first and second moments (the mean and the variance) alone. Asset returns are far from normal, however, and the mean and variance do not accurately describe the characteristics of an asset's return distribution.[35] For example, many risks and undesirable scenarios faced by a portfolio manager cannot be captured solely by the variance of the portfolio. As a result, in cases of significant nonnormality, the MVO approach will not be a satisfactory portfolio allocation model.

Considerable thought and innovation in the financial industry since the mid-1990s have been directed to bettering the profession's understanding of risk and its measurement and to improving the management of risk in financial portfolios. The main focus of this research is the ratio between the *bulk of the risk* and the *risk of the tails* of security return distributions.

One can distinguish between two types of risk measures: (1) dispersion and (2) downside risk.[36] Dispersion measures are measures of uncertainty—that is, of fluctuations on the upside and the downside. Standard deviation is one such measure. Downside risk measures, as the name implies, attempt to measure only deviations that have a negative impact. Most downside measures try to quantify an investment's probability of loss and/or severity of loss. An example is value at risk, which measures the predicted maximum loss at a specified probability level (95 percent, for instance) over a certain time horizon (say, 10 days).

The question is: When should one risk measure be used and not another? The short answer is: It depends. There is no "one size fits all" risk measure. On the one hand, a portfolio manager tracking the S&P 500 is concerned about *tracking error*—how much the portfolio is deviating (monthly, quarterly, yearly) from the index. Such tracking error is typically measured by the standard deviation of the difference

[34]See, for example, Alizadeh and Goldfarb (2003); Ben-Tal and Nemirovski (2001); Lobo, Vandenberghe, Boyd, and Lebret (1998). Chapters 6 and 9 of Fabozzi, Focardi, and Kolm (2006a) provide a more detailed discussion of the technical issues of robust portfolio optimization and a general overview of modern optimization algorithms.
[35]For a discussion of the empirical evidence, see Rachev, Menn, and Fabozzi (2005).
[36]See Rachev et al. (2005).

in return between the fund and the index.[37] On the other hand, a portfolio manager deploying sophisticated derivative strategies (for example, selling out-of-the-money equity put options) is going to be more worried about downside risk. In particular, this manager wants to be able to assess the likelihood of losing a certain amount of money when the market goes down.

The Myopic (One-Period) Framework. The Markowitz framework is a one-period-ahead framework. At every time step, the investor is concerned with returns at the end of and not beyond a single given period. Such a myopic framework does not take into consideration any decisions that might be made at the end of the period. A far-sighted framework anticipates the impact of decisions that will be made later, in the sense of a possible trade-off between returns at the end of the period and costs that might be incurred beyond the period.

If one believes that present decisions must be influenced by future trade-offs between returns and costs, the myopic framework is inappropriate. For example, if an investor forecasts that an asset will exhibit a positive return in the next period but negative returns in the following periods, the investor must consider transaction costs and liquidity risk at the next step, when the asset is likely to be sold. As a result, the investor might not invest in an asset that would look profitable at a one-period horizon. Hedge funds with high turnover are a typical instance of investors that might have to consider multiple periods ahead.

A myopic framework is also inappropriate when an investor has to optimize a consumption stream. In this case, the investor must consider the entire future path of consumption and returns. A pension fund has the opposite problem: The consumption stream (i.e., liability structure) is given but contributions and investment allocations need to be optimized. A myopic approach is also inappropriate in this case.[38]

The one-period-ahead framework is thus applicable to an investment environment characterized by low turnover, low transaction costs, little liquidity risk, and no stream of consumption or contributions to optimize. It is also generally applicable if returns are (at least approximately) IID sequences, although using the framework will nevertheless generate transaction costs because of rebalancing. The one-period-ahead framework will not allow one to forecast or, consequently, optimize costs from rebalancing or from any other type of transaction.

A far-sighted framework is the realm of multistage stochastic optimization, which requires the creation of a tree of scenarios up to the horizon at which the investor can reasonably make dynamic forecasts.[39] Multistage stochastic optimization is a complex technique, however, and is rarely used now in the industry.

---

[37]The typical annual tracking error of an S&P 500 index fund is 5–30 bps after fees.

[38]See, for example, Mulvey, Simsek, Zhang, Fabozzi, and Pauling (2005).

[39]For more on stochastic optimization and its application to asset management, see Ziemba (2003).

Rebalancing Portfolios. Portfolios need to be rebalanced when weights are no longer optimal, which can occur because (1) asset prices are subject to random fluctuations, (2) the forecast of returns has changed (if some predictability exists), or (3) model performance has changed. We consider each reason.

First, asset prices fluctuate randomly. If an investor assumes returns are IID variables, the *optimal* weights will be constant because they are determined by the time-invariant statistical properties of returns. The *actual* weights of any portfolio will fluctuate, however, and rebalancing will be necessary. When coupled with the CAPM framework, this situation creates a difficulty. In the CAPM, the optimal weights, which are constant, are always equal to the weights of the market portfolio; however, the weights of the market portfolio fluctuate.

Second, if the portfolio manager assumes predictability in asset expected returns or in the variance–covariance matrix, rebalancing will be necessary because risk and return forecasts change from period to period. The extent of the rebalancing that results from changing forecasts, however, can be predicted. For example, if the manager adopts a mean-reverting model, the manager knows that the forecast of returns will change when returns revert to the mean. Thus, the manager can estimate the timing of the change.

Third, the performance of the models themselves might change. These changes might be caused by predictable regime changes (e.g., rising interest rates) or unpredictable structural breaks. In practice, managers periodically reestimate their models on the basis of a moving window and change them in light of new information.

Because rebalancing portfolios entails transaction costs, optimizing the frequency of portfolio rebalancing is important. Various strategies can be adopted. *Calendar* rebalancing looks at portfolios at given dates and rebalances them on the basis of new estimates. *Threshold* rebalancing is applied when the portfolio weights differ from the optimal weights by more than a given threshold.

4. New Territory: Modeling for Portfolio and Tactical Asset Management

Arbitrage pricing theories preclude only situations of arbitrage; that is, they prevent the possibility of making a sure profit without an investment. The theories leave open the possibility of many active trading strategies based on the joint forecastability of risk and returns. The focus of this chapter is the models designed for the short time horizons typical of portfolio management and tactical asset management. These models enable the investor to make forecasts that depend on the present and past state of the market and are expected to be profitable over those horizons.[40] The time horizon of tactical asset management—the horizon for which forecasts are made and portfolios are rebalanced—ranges from a few days to a few months.

The first point to keep in mind is that a number of consequences of the capital asset pricing model (CAPM) are not in line with observations of the markets over short time horizons. In discussing this topic, we introduce some concepts that are important to understanding predictive models and their role in portfolio management and in tactical asset allocation. Specifically, we show how the belief that markets remunerate risk is incompatible with the hypothesis of the unforecastability of financial markets. In fact, the remuneration of risk implies that one can make an estimate of both risk and expected returns. Unless one believes that these estimates are static and valid for every future moment (which is unlikely), one has to admit that forecasts of expected returns are conditional on the present market situation—that is, markets must exhibit some predictability.

Active managers have always believed that markets are forecastable, although only through judgment and intuition backed by traditional financial analysis of individual companies, industries, or the economy. Market forecastability has been ascribed to mistakes the market makes in setting the prices of assets or to the "animal spirits" that drive markets. In contrast to these attitudes of active managers, mainstream finance theory has generally refused to admit market forecastability. Now, the availability of data and the speed and power of computers allow a scientific, quantitative evaluation of short-term market forecastability.

---

[40]Models that exhibit forecastability for the long time horizons typical of strategic asset allocation are discussed in Chapter 5.

The CAPM vs. Empirical Evidence

The CAPM was considered a major breakthrough when it was proposed in the 1960s by Treynor (1961), Sharpe (1964), Lintner (1965), and Mossin (1966). In introducing general equilibrium, the CAPM offered a formidable conceptual consolidation of asset-pricing theory. The merits and shortcomings of the CAPM have been widely discussed in the literature; our objective here is to show how a number of consequences of the CAPM (and of static factor models in general) are incompatible with empirical findings about stock price behavior. In particular, we discuss the consequences of the *two-fund separation theorem* and of the static risk-return remuneration implied by the CAPM.

The Two-Fund Separation Theorem. Asset managers who use mean-variance optimization expect to rebalance their portfolios periodically in light of changing market situations. However, if all investors behaved as mean-variance optimizers (as assumed by the CAPM), the market would be subject to an inconsistency. This inconsistency, as pointed out by Rosenberg and Ohlson (1976), is the consequence of the two-fund separation property.

The CAPM concludes that the only risk measure investors need to estimate is the beta of each asset—that is, the (scaled) covariance of that asset's returns with those of the market portfolio. This feature of the CAPM is attractive because it implies that the number of parameters that need to be estimated is proportional to the number of assets in a portfolio. If one had to take into consideration the mutual covariances between each pair of assets, the number of parameters to estimate would grow with the square of the number of assets, making estimates too numerous and too noisy. For example, in the case of the S&P 500 Index, the CAPM requires the estimation of 500 variances plus 500 betas (covariances scaled to the variance of the market portfolio). If all covariances had to be estimated, approximately 125,000 estimates would be needed.

The two-fund separation theorem states that if the market includes a risk-free asset, investors invest in a combination of only two "funds": the risk-free asset and the market portfolio. This statement, which can be analytically demonstrated in the context of the CAPM, was made by Tobin (1958) before the formulation of the CAPM. Tobin argued that investment is a two-stage process. The first stage is deciding how to build an efficient portfolio of risky assets. The second stage is the allocation of one's entire store of investment money between the efficient portfolio of risky assets and the risk-free asset.[41] This process is called "two-fund separation."

The two-fund separation theorem implies, however, that if the number of stocks remains constant, all stock prices must be perfectly collinear (i.e., perfectly

---

[41]The two-fund separation theorem can be generalized to *m* funds: An *m*-fund separation theorem holds if investors invest in *m* mutual funds. The conclusion that asset prices must be perfectly collinear remains unaltered.

correlated). In other words, there cannot be any relative price fluctuation. To see this implication intuitively, consider that Markowitz mean–variance optimization determines each investor's portfolio weights as a function of the statistical properties of asset returns. The CAPM explicitly assumes that investors behave as prescribed by the Markowitz theory. If the statistical properties of asset returns remain constant, as assumed by the CAPM, portfolio weights are also constant. Because all investors invest in the market portfolio, the market portfolio must have constant weights; that is, assets must be perfectly collinear.

But assets are not perfectly collinear. The prices of stocks fluctuate, so the perfect collinearity of stock prices does not hold. This conclusion can be avoided if we allow for the circumstance that the number of outstanding stocks is not constant. However, the fluctuations in the number of stocks are not of a magnitude sufficient to explain return fluctuations. Thus, the reader can see the inconsistency between a static market model and the concept of investors capable of discriminating expected returns and measures of risk.

Asset Pricing with Multiple Interacting Agents

In practice, investors are heterogeneous, make approximate forecasts (subject to error), and change their forecasts when new information arrives. The flow of information is not immediate and equal for all investors but reaches different investors at different moments; the reasons are differences in the diffusion, reception, and interpretation of data.

In practice, the same news item is received, interpreted, and acted upon differently by different investors (or market agents). For example, five new research documents come out of Wall Street every minute, and the asset managers at medium-sized firms receive up to 1,000 e-mails daily and work with as many as five screens on their desk (Intertek Group 2002). Even though data providers such as Factiva and FactSet Research Systems offer automatic systems that filter data according to criteria specified by the customer, agents are not number crunchers. Nor are agents perfectly rational. They communicate among themselves and are subject to mutual influences. They are subject to imitation (or herding) and other psychological or judgmental biases. In short, agents have only limited forecasting ability based on (partial) past data; they are *boundedly* rational agents.

Research on the behavior of markets as collections of heterogeneous and interacting agents began in earnest in the second half of the 1990s at the Santa Fe Institute under the direction of economist W. Brian Arthur.[42] This strain of research attempts to describe what happens to prices and returns under different

---

[42]The research was initially supported and funded by Citibank. John S. Reed, who was then CEO of Citibank and who was a chemical engineer by training, wanted to explore unconventional ways of using science to reinvent the bank.

characterizations of agent behavior. Arthur and his team built an artificial market to simulate the behavior of markets populated by interacting agents. Such simulations were (and still are) important because of the difficulty of analytically characterizing the behavior of large populations of heterogeneous agents.

A general conclusion of the many studies on heterogeneous interacting agents is that such agents form patterns of behavior—in particular, patterns of supply-and-demand behavior.[43] This conclusion seems counterintuitive if one expects that a multitude of boundedly rational agents would create random supply-and-demand patterns and thus uncertainty in investment behavior. Instead, at the aggregate level, a multitude of boundedly rational agents generally shows specific patterns of behavior and thus produces forecastability. That is, any multitude of boundedly rational agents exhibits a distribution of delayed responses. The interplay of these responses creates structure in market prices.

A number of short-term market price patterns have been empirically ascertained in financial markets. These patterns are the subject of the following section.

Market Feedbacks

Among the phenomena being modeled in an attempt to forecast equity returns are

* delayed response,
* momentum,
* reversal, and
* mean reversion and cointegration.

Delayed Response. The use of exogenous predictors to forecast equity returns is widely practiced in the industry for analyzing some market indices. It is the bread and butter of the modeling effort (see Chapter 11). From the point of view of market microstructure, the existence of predictors implies that agents exhibit a delayed response to new information: Clearly, if all agents reacted immediately to new information, no market predictor would exist; the effect of new information would be immediate.

For example, as documented in Campbell, Lo, and MacKinlay (1996) and, formally, in Kanas and Kouretas (2005), the market has price leaders and price laggards; specifically, the prices of large companies affect the prices of small companies, but the reverse does not occur.

Delays in response to new information are a result of one-way causal links (e.g., the price leader/laggard phenomenon) and the distribution of agent responses. As for distribution, consider the example of news breaking about a public company. Some information (such as increased profits) is immediately interpreted by all agents in a similar way and translated into an immediate change in the price of the

---

[43]For a good introduction to heterogeneous interacting agents, see Kirman (1994).

company's stock. Other news, however (such as a change in company president), might be interpreted differently and at a different pace by agents. These differences affect company financial ratios as predictors, and authors have various opinions on the subject.[44]

Momentum. The term "momentum" is used to describe both a market phenomenon and a trading strategy. Momentum strategies generally buy the past winners and sell the past losers. They rest on the idea that if a stock's price is rising, it will continue to rise, at least momentarily, and if a stock's price is falling, it will continue to fall. The existence of momentum effects can be explained quite naturally. If the financial markets are populated by agents who exhibit a delayed response to new information and are subject to mutual influence and if causal chains of influence do exist, then prices will naturally exhibit momentum.

The nature of behavioral patterns that lead to momentum profits has been investigated in the literature. Momentum effects are characterized by (1) the number of past time lags on which returns are evaluated and (2) the number of future time lags that form the prediction horizon. In their studies of the movement of stock prices, Jegadeesh and Titman (1993, 2001) found such momentum effects systematically for various horizons. Lewellen (2005) confirmed the finding of momentum in U.S. stock markets, and Rouwenhorst (1998) found momentum effects in European markets. We found (see Chapter 11) that momentum strategies occupy the second place after strategies based on predictors—such as company financial ratios or macroeconomic variables—that anticipate price movements. In analyzing possible sources of momentum (and contrarian) profit at the level of individual stocks and indices, these researchers found momentum for periods between 3 and 12 months when returns were measured over periods in the same range. Lo and MacKinlay (1990) proposed a convenient tool for analyzing whether momentum profits depend on individual momentum or on cross-autocorrelation effects.

The real challenge is not to prove the existence of momentum effects but to use momentum effects to implement profitable trading strategies. To construct momentum trading strategies that provide profits from large aggregates after transaction costs is relatively easy. Lo and MacKinlay (1990), for example, described one such strategy. The turnover suggested by the use of momentum strategies, however, is often excessive. This characteristic is one of the drawbacks mentioned by a number of sources in our survey. Practical implementation of momentum strategies requires some sort of optimization of momentum. This challenge is the realm of proprietary trading strategies.

---

[44]For this research, Bhargava and Malhotra (2006) use cointegration to give a definitive answer.

Reversal. Momentum and reversal are partners but appear at different time horizons. Where momentum exists, reversal must exist; prices cannot exhibit momentum—in one direction or another—*ad infinitum*. The same papers noted in the previous section that documented momentum also documented reversal. Momentum and reversal are thus well-documented phenomena, but the magnitude of the two phenomena and their time horizons in various markets differ considerably.

Reversal strategies are more difficult to implement than momentum strategies. Whereas momentum is a well-defined, *persistent* phenomenon, reversals are difficult to identify and to time precisely. For a strategy based on reversal, one has to identify or predict (with at least some degree of accuracy) the *moment* the direction in the trend of a stock price reverts.

Our survey showed that, although reversal strategies are being implemented, they are being used less than momentum strategies. Indeed, an advantage in implementing a reversal strategy is that because they are used less often, profitability from the strategy is less likely to be eroded by wide application.

Cointegration and Mean Reversion. Two or more time series are said to be cointegrated if they stay close together even if, individually, they behave as random walks. A pictorial illustration of cointegration is that of a drunken man walking his dog: Both wander aimlessly about, but the distance between the man and the dog fluctuates in a stationary way. Cointegrating relationships express long-run equilibrium between time series. As explained in Chapter 8, Bossaerts (1988) proposed cointegration as a possible solution to the inconsistencies of agents as mean–variance optimizers under the CAPM. As Chapter 8 shows, the existence of cointegration in asset *prices* (returns cannot be cointegrated because they are stationary) implies that a small number of common trends are at work in financial markets. If cointegration is present, price processes can be expressed as regressions on a restricted number of common stochastic (i.e., random) trends. In addition, one can construct stationary portfolios.

Cointegration is related to mean reversion. In fact, in a cointegrating relationship, one process reverts to the other(s). A classical question about the behavior of stock price processes is the presence (or absence) of mean reversion: Do stock prices fluctuate in the long run around some deterministic trend, or do they meander as a random walk? Meandering has been argued by, among others, Malkiel (1973). Empirical studies have found mixed evidence of random walk behavior and no strong evidence in favor of mean reversion (see Campbell, Lo, and MacKinlay 1996).

Again, from an asset manager's point of view, the key question is not whether cointegration exists in financial prices but whether there is sufficient cointegration for a trading strategy to yield profits. In practice, cointegrating relationships are difficult to identify in large sets of data, such as the individual stocks composing the S&P 500. The usual methodologies for testing and estimating cointegrating relationships are applicable only to a small number, in the range of 10–20, of processes. For this reason, cointegration has been exploited primarily at the level of pair trading—that is, applied to pairs of stocks—or to a small number of indices. (This approach does not, however, exploit the full potential of cointegration.) Moreover, successful use of cointegration typically relies on proprietary methods to identify cointegrating relationships and common trends.

Data and Model Complexity

Phenomena such as delayed response, momentum, reversal, and cointegration offer reasons to believe that financial markets are somehow predictable in the short term. (We look at the longer term in Chapter 5.) The question is: Can portfolio managers model the predictability to create a profitable strategy for the short term?

Predictive models are by nature *dynamic* models, not static models (like the CAPM). Other things being equal, predictive models include many more parameters than static models. For example, the number of parameters in a linear autoregressive model with two time lags is three times that of a random walk model. As we showed in Chapter 3, estimating a variance–covariance matrix is already so challenging that it calls for drastic reduction in the number of parameters. Clearly, estimating a dynamic model requires an even more significant reduction in the number of parameters.

The problem is that, as discussed in Chapter 7, from the point of view of modeling, the financial data are *scarce* and can support only simple models.[45] Therefore, in considering the transition from static to dynamic models—both of which are only approximations of reality—remember that only simple dynamic models can be realistically estimated. Modelers cannot simply add the complexity of dynamic relationships to static models. Using dynamic models involves a trade-off between the gain in terms of explanatory power and the loss in terms of estimation noise.

For example, suppose a manager has estimated 15 static factors to estimate a variance–covariance matrix; if the manager decides to determine the dynamic structure of the factors by using three lags, the manager will probably have to be content with only 3 of the 15 factors because of insufficient data for estimating a dynamic model of the factors.

Transaction Costs and Profitability

The possibility of forecasting financial markets does not necessarily translate into profitable trading strategies. In fact, an apparently profitable forecast may entail increased risk and transaction costs that can wipe out profits. Consider, for example,

---

[45]The assertion of a scarcity of data may sound strange in light of the apparent superabundance of financial data, but statistically, it is correct.

a long–short equity strategy that offers the prospect of a substantial profit, although with substantial residual risk. If the apparent profitability of the strategy disappears in practice, the reason is often that transaction costs are larger than anticipated.

In accounting for transaction costs, a manager must consider both the cost charged by the broker to perform transactions and the impact of the trades on prices. Thus, strategies requiring heavy trading or involving the stocks of small companies are often much less profitable in practice than in a backtest or simulation that does not account for transaction costs.

Transaction costs also increase the difficulty of understanding the risk–return profile of dynamic models. In a predictive environment with transaction costs, the one-period mean–variance framework is no longer applicable. The reason is that at every moment, the investor must take into account that decisions will be revised at a later date at an associated cost. Suppose, for example, that a model forecasts a significant positive expected return of a given asset in one period followed by a negative expected return in the following period. An investor has to weigh the expected profit from investing in the asset in the first period against the cost of investing and then disinvesting in an ensuing period. These situations are typical of cointegration-based strategies, in which the stationary mean-reverting behavior of cointegrating portfolios calls for frequent rebalancing.

The consideration of transaction costs in far-sighted asset management calls for optimization over multiple future periods. Optimization methods that consider multiple periods are called "multistage stochastic optimization methods." They typically work by (1) creating scenarios representative of all possible situations and (2) assigning a probability to each scenario.

The problem is that stochastic optimization is cumbersome and computationally intensive. In realistic applications, the number of scenarios to be considered can reach thousands. Our survey of asset managers (see Chapter 11) found that none were presently using the technique.[46]

Conclusion

The predictability of expected returns and risk allows one to solve a number of inconsistencies that have been found in purely static models of returns. Among the market phenomena that allow the forecasting of equity returns and risk are delayed response, momentum, reversal, and cointegration. These phenomena are being addressed with dynamic models that we discuss in Chapters 6 and 8.

---

[46]In a 2004 study on modeling at pension funds in the Netherlands, Switzerland, the United Kingdom, and the United States, Fabozzi, Focardi, and Jonas (2005) found that, although multistage stochastic optimization was being widely used on the asset/liability management side by consultants, most large Dutch funds preferred simulation to optimization.

Two problems emerge, however, in the use of dynamic models: (1) a scarcity of financial data and (2) hurdles to implementing profitable trading strategies. The scarcity of data is the key limiting factor. Although overabundant from the human point of view, data are insufficient to estimate complex models. The existence of predictability in itself is not sufficient to guarantee profitable trading strategies. Risk and transaction costs can nullify the profit of apparently sound trading strategies. Careful consideration of risk–return trade-offs and costs is needed to ensure that market predictability results in profitable trading.

5. New Territory: Forecastability and the Long-Term Perspective

In the previous chapter, we discussed the economic basis of market forecastability from the perspective of the short time horizon typical of portfolio management and of tactical asset allocation. In this chapter, we discuss market forecastability from the perspective of a longer time horizon. We approach the question of profitable long-term forecastability from the perspective of robust modeling as defined in previous chapters. We do so by first considering some important questions encountered in shifting the time perspective from the short term to the long term. We then briefly discuss the modeling of long-term stock price or stock index behavior.

Shifting Time Perspectives

We begin by considering four questions that arise when one shifts from a short-term to a long-term perspective:

- How does market behavior aggregate over time?
- Can one assume that patterns of market behavior are the same at short and long time horizons?
- Can one recognize *regime shifts* (i.e., reversals in trends)?
- Can practitioners use approximate models, estimating them on moving data windows across time (e.g., January 1999–December 2004, February 1999–January 2005, and so on)?

Answering these questions is not easy, but at least a partial response is required to determine just what phenomena can be modeled and with what techniques. The practice of estimating models on a moving window, for example, rests on important assumptions about the long-term behavior of the models being estimated. We use the following section to take a close look at each of the questions posed.

Aggregation over Time. The first question deals with how market behavior aggregates over time, an issue that has been widely considered in the literature. The first thing to do in discussing the question is to define the concept of *time aggregation*. Suppose that we have daily stock price data or return data and that we have a model of the evolution of prices through time. Consider now that we want to apply the model to different time spans—for example, hourly intervals and monthly intervals. Can the same model be applied to the short as well as the long time intervals? The answer, generally speaking, is no. For example, an autoregressive process with an autocorrelation period of a few days becomes (approximately) an independent and identically distributed (IID) sequence at monthly intervals. Or a series might look approximately IID at short time intervals but exhibit an autocorrelated structure at long time intervals. For example, a random walk with very slow periodic fluctuations in its average growth rate (e.g., its average growth rate fluctuates slowly between 3 percent and 4 percent) will be indistinguishable from a random walk at short time intervals but is forecastable at a longer time horizon.

Processes that do look the same for different time aggregations are called "self-similar." And the simplest process that is invariant after time aggregation is the random walk. One of the reasons models of self-similar behavior—such as chaos, nonlinear dynamics, and fractals—have attracted so much attention in the past several decades is that they are self-similar after time aggregation.[47]

In the 1960s, Benoît Mandelbrot, a mathematician working at the IBM Thomas J. Watson Research Center in Yorktown Heights, New York, observed that many price–time series, including the price of cotton over time, have descriptions that do not depend on the scale of the measurements and these descriptions are often self-replicating or self-similar (see, e.g., Mandelbrot 1963). In other words, Mandelbrot observed that the time series of *daily* cotton prices is practically indistinguishable from the series of *monthly* cotton prices. Since Mandelbrot's observation, the hypothesis of the self-similarity of stock prices has been widely debated. If prices follow a random walk, then they are self-similar.[48]

Most long-term predictive models currently in use are not self-similar but exhibit a well-defined time scale. Regressive and autoregressive models (see Chapter 7) have a time scale given by the time horizon at which correlations and autocorrelations decay. The generalized autoregressive conditional heteroscedasticity (GARCH) family of models has a time scale and does not remain invariant after time aggregation. Regime-shift models also exhibit a time scale.

The ability to aggregate time and to use models developed and calibrated on a short horizon for long horizons would be extremely useful. It would allow researchers not only to study long-term market behavior from, say, daily data, but also to take advantage of high-frequency data for portfolio management, to make useful forecasts, or to make more accurate estimates of the variance–covariance matrix than are now possible. Consider that Falkenberry (2002) estimated that the median stock in the Russell 3000 Index produces approximately 2,100 ticks

---

[47]Such self-similar models are not frequently used in asset management, although they are used in several other disciplines, such as the analysis of communication traffic. For a survey, see Samorodnitsky and Taqqu (1994).

[48]Although an arithmetic random walk with normal increments is a self-similar process, there are also self-similar processes with nonnormal distributions that are thus more complicated than the random walk.

per day (530,000 per year). If we could use high-frequency data, we would have access to databases 2,000-fold larger than the usual daily databases.[49]

Market Behavior at Different Time Horizons. From an economic point of view, the long-run behavior of stock prices is influenced by factors different from those that influence their short-term behavior. At time horizons of days or weeks, trading practices and the way traders react to news are primarily responsible for asset price predictability; in the long run, the price of an individual asset is determined not only by the financial performance of the company but also by the quantity of money in the market and the global performance of the economy. Rapidly expanding financial markets require rapidly expanding monetary flows, which are eventually selectively channeled. Thus, from a long-term perspective, the monetary policies of central banks play a key role in determining market performance. As for the global performance of the economy (domestic and worldwide), the formation of economic areas characterized by extensive innovation favors the creation of a rapidly expanding quantity of money with minimal impact on inflation.[50]

In the long run, prices are unlikely to behave as correlated random walks with different rates of drift. If they did, the result would be exponentially diverging price processes and, ultimately, the concentration of the economy in one or a limited number of companies. But as is well known, neither the distribution of stock prices nor the distribution of market capitalization decays exponentially. Actually, it has been empirically ascertained that the market capitalization of companies follows a Pareto law and does not decay exponentially.[51]

Determining whether financial markets behave the same over short time horizons as they do over long time horizons would require homogeneous data, and researchers do not have such data. Being open systems, financial markets are continuously changing, with new companies entering and others exiting or merging. Moreover, although detailed stock price data are available for about one century, the structure of the stock market has changed significantly during that period. At the end of the 19th century, far fewer companies were listed on the New York Stock Exchange than at the end of the 20th century. Clearly, simple tests of similarity of market behavior are meaningless.

---

[49]See Mantegna and Stanley (1999) for a survey of the status of research in this area.

[50]In modern times, monetary expansion without significant inflation is typically related to technological innovation, but such a relationship is by no means the only possibility. For example, in the 1300–1600 period in Italy, consumption patterns changed significantly (and the economy developed rapidly) with the new demand for art in all its forms—architecture, sculpture, painting, objets d'art, and domestic furnishings—by both the clergy and secular society. See Goldthwaite (1995).

[51]Pareto's law states that there is a linear relationship between the logarithms of income, I, and the number of people that earn more than I (see also Chapter 2). Axtell (2001) confirmed that the Pareto law applies to market capitalization across all U.S. companies.

Although it might seem plausible for the behavior of financial markets to be different at different time horizons, the high level of noise in financial market prices (i.e., the numerous fluctuations that models do not explain) makes it difficult to draw definite conclusions. The models that asset management firms use do not differ much for different time horizons, although their parameterizations change significantly.

Recognizing Regime Shifts. A key question in modeling for long time horizons is whether feedback is continuous or of a more discrete nature. Do markets adjust continuously, or do they follow a given regime and then switch suddenly to another regime—or do they do a bit of both? Discrete changes call for a modeling strategy in which market behavior is approximated *piecewise* in relatively simple models. Regime shifts of a discrete nature can be set off by exogenous changes (for example, monetary policy changes) or by particular endogenous situations that trigger significant change (such as the crash of October 1987). In the strategies for modeling regime shifts, there is no clear-cut separation between the two because both are approximations of reality.

The need to model regime shifts arises from the fact that our models are only simplified approximations. Researchers use simple models to approximate real market behavior and adjust the models to fit empirical data by allowing the model parameters to change. Modelers introduce auxiliary (typically, nonobservable or hidden) variables that represent regimes, or "state variables."[52,53] In some cases, regimes seem to have a clear economic interpretation. For example, the recession/ expansion cycles seem to be a clear economic reality. In other cases, the economic interpretation is difficult, perhaps impossible.

Actually, whether regime shifts are continuous or discrete is not clear. The answer hinges, ultimately, on which models best describe economic reality. For example, GARCH models and Hamilton models represent the clustering of, respectively, volatility and drift. That is, the GARCH model represents the fact that periods of high volatility are followed by periods of low volatility, whereas the Hamilton model represents the fact that periods of economic growth are followed by periods when the economy does not grow or shrinks. GARCH models posit a continuous regime shift; the Hamilton model, a discrete regime shift. In Chapter 7, we briefly describe a number of models that implement regime shifts. Whether one should adopt one or another model is an empirical question.

---

[52]Modeling strategies of this type are often used in the physical sciences. For example, the development of thermodynamics progressively introduced new variables that were not directly observable. Einstein, who did not like the uncertain nature of quantum mechanics, argued that quantum mechanics could be explained by adding hidden variables. This approach is the so-called EPR conjecture (named after its proponents Einstein, Podolsky, and Rosenberg).

[53]For a discussion of these models, see Chapter 16 in Fabozzi, Focardi, and Kolm (2006a).

Estimating Approximate Models on Moving Windows. Is estimating approximate models on moving windows (i.e., on periods of time that move) legitimate? If so, what errors might thereby be introduced?

Estimating models on a moving window is a current practice in modeling. On the one hand, if regime shifts are gradual and continuous, estimating models on a moving window will be an approximation without major shifts. On the other hand, if regime shifts are sharp, models will perform well until the moment of the shift, and then, their performance will degrade abruptly.

Unlike the problem of the stability of market behavior at different time horizons, researchers can, with appropriate tests, detect regime breaks. The question is what to do after a break has been detected and the models have not yet learned the new parameters. Methodologies such as those described in Chapter 8 should help.

Modeling Long-Term Behavior

How do researchers model the long-term behavior of financial markets? Recall that a static model is a model in which relationships do not depend on the past. The CAPM is such a model: It computes a stock's excess return as a function of the market portfolio excess return and the covariability of the stock with the market portfolio. Static relationships of this type cannot be long-term models of stock prices. Empirical research has ascertained that there are different levels of covariability between stocks and the market portfolio. The implication is that static models of the market exhibit exponentially diverging price processes.

The same conclusion (i.e., that exponentially diverging price processes exist) holds if one assumes that returns are multivariate-correlated, IID variables. This assumption is made in, for example, the arbitrage pricing theory model formulated by Ross (1976), in which each stock return is a weighted average of a number of factors. Although the no-arbitrage condition restricts the eventual intercept term—the alpha—the existence of assets with different risk levels means that expected excess returns can be different for different assets, as in the univariate CAPM. In the long run, different expected excess returns produce exponentially diverging price processes.

This discussion leads to the conclusion that static models of returns cannot serve to model the long term. To appreciate this point, we simulated a market portfolio random walk process for a period of 30 years. We assumed a 4 percent yearly excess return over a 3 percent yearly risk-free rate, and we generated 10,000 individual random walks representing 10,000 different stocks. Each process was specified according to the CAPM, with levels of beta uniformly distributed from 0.5 to 2. The starting stock price was set to 1.0 for all processes. **Figure 5.1** gives a bird's eye view of the behavior of the stocks' cumulative returns over the 30-year period. The heavy line represents the market portfolio and the lighter lines and area are the area filled by the 10,000 random walk paths. The exponential growth of the

Figure 5.1. Behavior of 10,000 Random Walk Paths

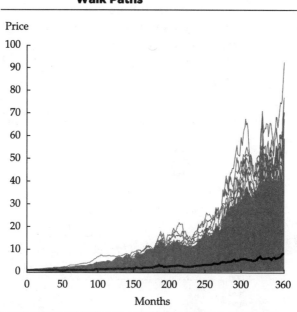

spread is visually clear. The three panels of **Figure 5.2** represent the distribution of prices at 10 years, 15 years, and 30 years. Clearly, the distribution of prices is approximately lognormal at 10 years but tends progressively to an exponential distribution over time.

Static models of returns are not reasonable long-term models of returns because they cannot capture changes in the markets or in individual companies. Public companies experience various vicissitudes during their lives, and the market changes its evaluation of companies, the economy, and market segments over time.

So, can dynamic models be considered reasonable long-term models? The answer to this question hinges on exactly what type of dynamic model(s) are to be used, and the answer elucidates some of the fundamental questions about modeling the long term. In a dynamic model, the distribution of prices or returns at a next step (i.e., the forecast) depends on present and past prices and returns. In general, researchers consider only a small number of past returns (or time lags); otherwise, estimation becomes too noisy.

Can dynamic models capture long-term regime shifts? This question is treated in detail in Chapter 7; here, it suffices to say that if only linear models are considered, the answer is no: A linear dynamic model cannot capture long-term regime shifts. It can only (eventually) capture oscillations or decay of a long duration. Linear models can capture only periodic movements with a fixed period.

Figure 5.2. Distribution of Prices

A. At 10 Years

Number of Points per Bin

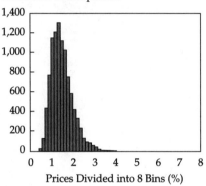

Prices Divided into 8 Bins (%)

B. At 15 Years

Number of Points per Bin

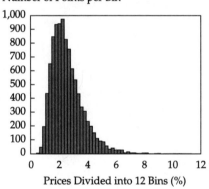

Prices Divided into 12 Bins (%)

C. At 30 Years

Number of Points per Bin

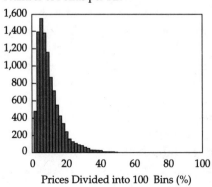

Prices Divided into 100 Bins (%)

The more complex *nonlinear* dynamic models can capture a broad variety of behavior, but to be useful, this complexity must be "tamed." Nonlinear models may exhibit chaotic behavior—oscillating behavior without any fixed periodicity. Unfortunately, despite efforts in the past two decades, representing economic behavior as deterministic nonlinear chaos has been impossible.

A class of models that has proved useful is the nonlinear *coupling* of two dynamic models. The coupling is obtained by making the parameters of the principal model a function of another, auxiliary model. The best known of these models is the GARCH family. Other vector autoregressive models that belong to this category include the Hamilton model and the Markov models (both discussed in Chapter 7).

A fundamental difficulty with nonlinear dynamic models is that they require the coupling of very different time constants. The principal model captures the dynamics of prices or returns that fluctuate over short time periods—say, days or even shorter periods. The auxiliary model must capture regime shifts, which might have a time horizon of months, years, or even decades. Additional difficulties arise if the regime shifts are to be considered endogenous (that is, at least partly a function of other parameters and variables in the model).

Mean Reversion

Whether market returns are mean reverting has been widely discussed in the literature. In this section, we discuss the following three questions that are important in modeling as it regards mean reversion:

- How does the compounding of returns affect mean reversion?
- How is the central trend to be defined?
- How does mean reversion affect time diversification?

Compounding and Mean Reversion. Mean reversion exists if the autocorrelation coefficient of the logarithm of the indices is less than 1. (If the autocorrelation coefficient is equal to 1, the process is a random walk. If the correlation is less than 1, the process oscillates around a linear trend.) A number of early studies found some evidence of mean reversion in the stock markets—in particular, Fama and French (1988), Lo and MacKinlay (1988), and Poterba and Summers (1988). These studies tested two hypotheses that the index behaves (1) as a random walk or (2) as a stationary process oscillating around a linear trend. Kim, Nelson, and Startz (1991), testing similar hypotheses, concluded that in the U.S. stock market, mean reversion is a pre–World War II phenomenon. Risager (1998) studied mean reversion in the Danish stock market following World War I with similar criteria and found evidence of mean reversion, especially in modern times.

All these studies were performed with the use of some version of the *variance ratio test*. This test is based on the fact that in a random walk, the variance grows proportionally with time. If the variance grows less rapidly than time, then the process is mean reverting. In other words, in a mean-reverting process, risk cancels itself out over time to some degree, whereas in a non-mean-reverting process, it does not.[54]

If the logarithms of prices behave as a stationary process with a linear trend, they are "trend stationary." That is, the prices themselves fluctuate around exponential trends. The standard deviation of prices—the dispersion around the trend—grows exponentially at the same rate as the trend. Note the fundamental difference between a trend-stationary process and a random walk with a linear trend. The variance of a random walk keeps on growing with time, but the variance of a trend-stationary process remains constant. **Figure 5.3** illustrates 50 paths of a trend-stationary process. The paths appear as the grey area of constant width around the black mean. **Figure 5.4** shows the mean and standard deviation for the trend-stationary process of Figure 5.3. Because the process is trend stationary, the mean grows linearly whereas the standard deviation remains approximately constant. **Figure 5.5** shows the corresponding exponential paths. The grey area represents the 50 paths; note that the width grows exponentially. **Figure 5.6** shows the mean (the thick line) and

Figure 5.3.   Fifty Paths of Trend-Stationary Process

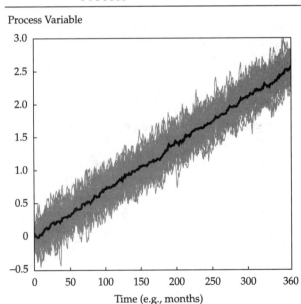

---

[54]The variance ratio test, with its associated sampling distributions and critical values, is discussed in Cochrane (1988) and Lo and MacKinlay (1988).

Figure 5.4. Mean and Standard Deviation of Trend-Stationary Process in Figure 5.3

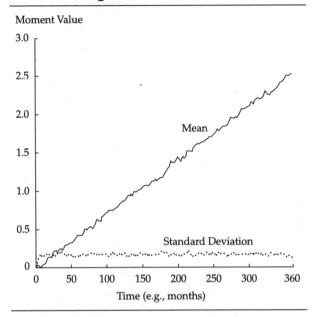

Figure 5.5. Exponential Processes Corresponding to 50 Paths of Figure 5.3

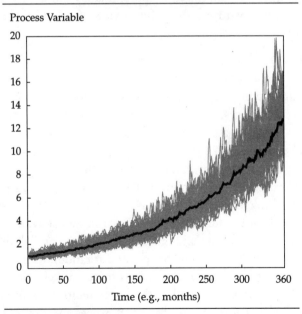

Figure 5.6. Mean and Standard Deviation of the Exponential Processes

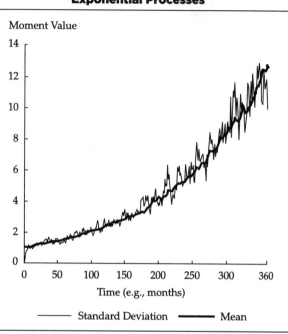

Moment Value

Time (e.g., months)

——— Standard Deviation   ▬▬ Mean

the standard deviation (the thin line) of the exponential processes. Note that the mean and the standard deviation follow approximately the same exponential path. These aspects are important from the point of view of risk management, as shown in the next section.

Defining the Central Tendency. Mean reversion of the logarithms of prices means that the logarithms of prices are stationary with a linear trend. Mean reversion, as defined previously, is interpreted as a property of single stock prices or, more commonly, indices. Actually, mean reversion can be articulated in three properties: (1) Stock prices are stationary around some trend; (2) trends are linear; (3) trends are all equal.

The property of stationarity around a linear trend can be generalized to cover the case of stationarity around nonlinear deterministic trends, stochastic trends, and stochastically broken trends. *Nonlinear deterministic trends* are trends that follow nonlinear behavior—for example, a logarithmic behavior. *Stochastic trends* are trends that are not deterministic but are subject to a probability distribution. *Stochastically broken trends* are trends that change at random times. The possibility of identifying nonlinear deterministic trends is quite unlikely. Stationarity around a stochastic trend has been proposed as the permanent/transitory model initially proposed by Muth (1960). In this model, stock prices are formed by a long-term random walk plus a short-term, transitory stationary adjustment. Broken-trend models include the Markov switching models, which handle different regimes and thus different trends.[55]

Given that a stock price process can be mean reverting around many different trends, the next question is: Does the entire market exhibit only one trend, or do many trends coexist? As shown previously, if the logarithms of prices behave in the long run as stationary processes with a linear trend, the linear trend must be the same for all processes. If not, the market would reflect an exponential spread of prices and thus of market capitalizations, but in practice, we find only a Pareto law of market capitalization. If trends involve some stochastic element, the question is more complex. A reasonable assumption is that if regime shifts can occur, each regime must be unique. The implication for practitioners is that in the long run, stock prices can have only one linear or stochastic trend.

These questions are presently not well discussed in the literature. The key problem is data. The data are insufficient to analyze multiple regime shifts—especially considering that in the long run, companies start, close, and undergo mergers and acquisitions. The tests of mean reversion have so far tested only one specific behavior—namely, mean reversion around a linear trend.

Time Diversification. "Time diversification" is the term given to the concept that stocks are less risky in the long run than in the short run. Based on time diversification, proponents of life-cycle investing suggest that in the early stages of life, one should take more risk (say, by investing in stocks) and later, when approaching retirement age, one should reduce risk by increasing one's allocation to bonds. Whether time diversification is a valid principle has been the subject of heated debate. Samuelson (1994), Bodie (1995), and Kritzman (1994, 1997) have argued that time diversification is not a valid investment principle. Thorley (1995) and Vanini and Vignola (2002) have argued that time diversification may be valid. Kritzman and Rich (2002) introduced a new perspective in the time diversification debate by arguing that investors should be concerned with the distributions of wealth at *intermediate* as well as final periods. Fabozzi, Focardi, and Kolm (forthcoming 2006b) observed that time diversification should be quantitatively measured as the ratio of a measure of risk to expected return.

As noted in this chapter, if in the long run the logarithms of prices are assumed to be stationary with linear trends, then prices themselves will exhibit a constant ratio of standard deviation (risk) to the mean return. That is, multiplicative compounding of returns implies that financial markets exhibit an approximately constant ratio of global risk to global return—that is, the reward expected per unit of risk is the same no matter what time horizon is being considered. Therefore, because of the compounding of returns, markets are unlikely to exhibit time diversification.

---

[55]Nielsen and Olesen (2000) investigated mean reversion with regime shifts in the Danish market.

Summary

The question of market forecastability from the perspective of a long time horizon must address several issues, including the aggregation of market behavior over different time spans, regime shifts, and the estimation of approximate models on moving windows. In analyzing the appropriate models to use for modeling market behavior over the long term (time horizons beyond a few months), we made the following points:

- Static models cannot be long-term models because permanent differences in the expected returns of different assets would lead to exponentially diverging market capitalizations.
- Linear dynamic models cannot be long-term models because their solutions allow only for exponential decay or periodic oscillations.
- Nonlinear dynamic models can be long-term models, but they are prone to intractable chaotic behavior.
- Coupling nonlinear dynamic models to represent both the short term and the long term might offer a solution, but simultaneously estimating short-term and long-term dynamics is a problem.
- Time diversification is the property by which risk (uncertainty) is less in long-term forecasts than in short-term forecasts. We believe that because of the geometric compounding of returns, time diversification does not exist in the market, even if the logarithms of prices are trend stationary. If the logarithms of prices are trend stationary with a linear trend, then prices evolve as exponentials and their standard deviations remain approximately proportional to the level of prices.

6. Machine Learning

The *machine-learning* approach to financial modeling is an attempt to find financial models automatically—without any theoretical assumptions—through a process of progressive adaptation. Machine learning is rooted in statistics and artificial intelligence (AI). We begin by commenting on two key concepts—learning and problem solving. Then, we describe several machine-learning approaches to automatic problem solving that play a role in asset management.

Machine learning (and AI techniques in general) is one of the many techniques used in specific applications in financial modeling. In the 1990s, AI and its application to financial forecasting generated a lot of exaggerated claims and hype and received a lot of professional and media attention. AI was considered a revolutionary technology that could completely change the way people were doing business in finance. Today, as noted by one of the pioneers in the application of AI to finance, David Leinweber, those days are over. The hyperbole has made way for a more pragmatic attitude: AI is useful, but its merits and limits are now more clearly understood (see Leinweber and Beinart 1996).

Concepts of Learning

The term "learning" assumes different meanings in different contexts. In our daily life, we use the concept of learning in two senses. In one sense, learning indicates an increase of knowledge, the conscious acquisition of a mental model. In this sense, a student learns literature at school, for example. We also use learning in another sense—that of acquiring a habit. This concept of learning is not restricted to any notion of a mental model. For example, when we learn to ride a bicycle, we acquire the right motor reflexes without any cognitive intermediation.

Machine learning is based on this second concept of learning. Learning is seen as a process of *progressive adaptation* that can be described in purely mechanical terms. In a general sense, learning is considered to be the ability to produce the right patterns in response to a given set of inputs. In principle, this notion of learning includes such high-level mental activities as automatic language translation.

How to formally represent the process of adapting the behavior of a machine (or an animal) to some target has been the subject of several decades of study. In machine learning, two fundamental forms of learning are distinguished: supervised and unsupervised learning.

Supervised Learning. In machine learning, supervised learning is learning from examples. From a number of approximately correct examples of pairs of output patterns and input stimuli, the machine learns how to respond to future stimuli. For example, machines that recognize human handwriting associate the correct sequence of letters (the output) to handwritten words (the stimuli). Machines are trained by showing them a number of handwritten patterns and the associated correct letters or words.

In more abstract terms, supervised learning is defined as *learning a function about which one has a number of approximate examples*. For example, the data-generation process (DGP) of a time series of prices is a *function* that links future returns with present and past returns. If only two lags are used, the DGP that we want to learn is the function, if it exists, that links prices at time $t + 1$ with prices at time t and $t - 1$. The sample in this case will be all the "triples" formed by prices in three consecutive instants for all the sample set. The sample is formed by approximate realizations of the DGP.

Supervised learning thus means approximation of a function for which a number of samples are known. In this sense, learning is equivalent to fitting a curve to a set of points. Many learning methods, however, work by *rules* that adapt a model progressively to new samples, a process that is different from usual curve fitting. The notion of learning is often associated with specific learning rules. For example, neural network learning is often associated with the *backpropagation algorithm* (discussed later), which is a learning rule. The two notions of "learning" and "learning rules" are potentially confusing and should be clearly distinguished.

Unsupervised Learning. Unsupervised learning is more difficult to define and understand than supervised learning. In unsupervised learning, a system discovers the structure of data through a process of *endogenous evolution*. Clustering is the typical example of unsupervised learning. One starts with a set of points and discovers the grouping of points into clusters.

In principle, the method of unsupervised learning applies to all available data. One can apply unsupervised learning to a sample, however, and then generalize to the entire population. For example, a financial application performs clustering of price–time series on sample data and then applies the same clustering to new data.

Statistical Learning. Supervised learning as defined here is the process of approximating a function from examples. The key ingredients in this concept are (1) a mathematical model able to approximate any function and (2) a set of rules for the approximation process from examples.

The concept of supervised learning does not, in itself, include any notion of prediction or generalization. The main objective of a considerable body of research has been to show that specific learning rules can effectively learn any pattern. Learning patterns of small samples with high precision, however, produces poor generalization and forecasting results for the population from which the sample came.

The approach that places the learning process in the context of generalization and forecasting is *statistical learning*. Given an efficient process of learning, statistical learning deals with how one can make sure that the learning process has good generalization and forecasting abilities.

Statistical learning attempts to answer this question in a probabilistic framework. Classical learning theory places limits on the model complexity in order to improve the forecasting capabilities of learned models. It does so by adding a penalty function that constrains model complexity. Vapnik (1995, 1998) introduced an important conceptual novelty by showing that not only does the complexity of the model matter but so also does the type of functions used. He was able to construct a mathematical framework to predict how well a given set of approximating functions would generalize.

Problem Solving

One area of AI deals with solving problems automatically. In this approach, the problem is specified by some general objective and the problem solver must synthesize the solution. For example, automatic methods have been applied to a typical problem in financial modeling—the design of new factor models.

The concept and techniques of problem solving evolved in the 1960s. In 1960, Herbert Simon forcefully expressed the notion that human decision-making processes can be automated through computational processes. The idea that a computer, which acts according to preprogrammed instructions, can exhibit creative power is difficult to believe. The link between algorithmic processes—that is, the step-by-step processes of computers—and creative problem solving is the concept of *searching*.

Automatic problem solving is based on the concept that human decision making and problem solving are ultimately the guided exploration of a set of predetermined possibilities. Automatic problem solving works by searching a "space," or "ensemble," of opportunities and choosing according to some criterion. Problem solving entails (1) the ability to describe the set of various possibilities, (2) a quantitative way to rate various solutions, and (3) a search and optimization strategy. Ultimately, problem solving is an application of optimization.[56]

Problem-solving methodologies have also been tackled from a different point of view. In exploring a vast set of opportunities, the temptation is to use probabilistic methods. John Holland (1976) had the idea of using probabilistic searches in the

---

[56] Several difficulties are associated with this concept of problem solving. As defined here, problem solving can search only a solution that already exists, at least conceptually. Much of human problem solving, however, is the definition of new concepts. How searches could find genuinely new concepts is not obvious. In addition, it was discovered that many apparently simple problems in daily life involve searching an *infinite* space. This is the so-called *frame problem* of AI.

context of genetic evolution. Holland reasoned that genetic evolution in biology seems to be an efficient probabilistic exploration device to find optimal solutions. From this idea, genetic algorithms were born.

Clearly, some of the concepts of AI—in particular, learning and problem solving—are continuations of the methodologies that have been used in statistics for more than a century. In the following sections, we discuss a number of machine-learning tools and some of their applications.

Neural Networks

From the point of view of financial modeling, artificial neural networks (ANNs) are universal function approximators. ANNs, however, have been studied from the general point of view of connectionist structures able to imitate some of the functions of the brain. It is useful to separate the two areas. As we stated earlier, AI has been surrounded by a lot of hype. The hype created, in turn, a lot of disappointment, because results were inferior to expectations. Much of the hype resulted from the fact that it was often assumed that AI was about building artificial brains with humanlike cognitive capabilities. In particular, although the properties of ANNs as nonlinear function approximators are well established, the possibilities that large ANNs exhibit cognitive abilities similar to a human brain is far from being demonstrated.

Basically, neural networks are machine-learning tools that can be used either in a supervised or an unsupervised mode. In a supervised mode, a neural network is used to learn a function from samples—for example, the DGP of a series from its past realization.

A neural network in a computer program for financial applications is formed by *nodes* and *connections*. Nodes are placed in multiple layers. The number of layers and the number of nodes in each layer are arbitrary. Nodes in one layer are connected only to nodes in the layers immediately below or above. A node receives inputs from the nodes in the layer below. Inputs are weighted, in the sense that each connection has an associated weight. The output of each node depends on the sum of the weighted inputs. If the sum of the inputs is below a given threshold, the output is zero; if it is above the threshold, the output is a given fixed value. When the network is in operation, inputs are applied to the lowest layer and propagate to the highest layer. Typically, the inputs represent one or more binary numbers and the output represents one binary number. But many configurations are possible.

The parameters to be learned are the weights. During the training phase—that is, during the learning process—both the inputs and the outputs are known. The objective is to determine the weights. **Figure 6.1** illustrates the schema of an ANN.

In general, in financial applications, neural networks are implemented as computer programs. In technological applications, neural networks are often implemented as stand-alone electronic devices. In this latter implementation, the neural network is trained offline and then physically implemented as an electronic circuit.

Figure 6.1. Schema of a Neural Network with Input Layer, Output Layer, and Hidden Layer of Neurons

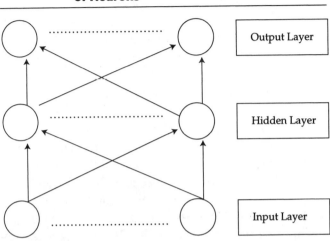

If the number of nodes and connections, and thus the number of weights, is unrestricted, one can fit any function with arbitrary precision.[57] The number of layers and nodes has to be restricted, however, to capture some true feature of the data. Many criteria and heuristics are available for choosing the right number of nodes and layers, but no constructive methodology exists. Designing a neural network is thus a question of intuition, trial and error, and testing.

Once the network *topology*—that is the number of nodes and their connections—has been fixed, one can estimate the weights by using either an optimizer or a specific learning procedure, such as backpropagation. An optimizer is a computer program that finds the maximum or minimum of a function. It considers all input–output sample data at the same time. First, one computes the errors as a function of the weights. The optimizer finds those weights that minimize errors. This process is similar to least-squares estimation. In backpropagation, input data are sequentially fed to the network and weights are updated as a function of output data. Backpropagation is an adaptive process: One starts with an initial guess of the weights, and the guess is progressively modified as a function of new data.

Neural networks can also be used in an unsupervised mode. A typical such application is *vector quantization*—a process that tries to find prototypes of a set of items. Suppose, for example, that one is given a set of companies defined by their financial ratios. The objective is to create a set of prototype companies so that each company is associated with a prototype.

---

[57]The proof of this statement was given by Cybenko (1989).

To perform vector quantization with neural networks, one has to know in advance the number of prototypes. Given that number, one uses a network with as many outputs as prototypes. All data are explored sequentially. Every time a new piece of data is acquired, the learning process selects the output that is the closest to the new data and slightly adjusts the weights of that output. At the end of the process, the weights of each network output represent a prototype.

Typically, neural networks are black boxes: Finding an interpretation of the weights is practically impossible. The only justification of a neural network comes from its testing. Rigorous testing methodologies are required.

In addition to the traditional neural network, numerous variants of networklike topology and training methods have been suggested. Hertz, Krogh, and Palmer (1991) provide an introduction to the mathematical theory of neural computation.

Neural networks have been widely applied in trading and portfolio management. Initially used as a new paradigm in forecasting, neural networks are now routinely used as nonlinear regressions. Our survey showed (see Chapter 11) that a number of asset management firms are quite happy with ANN applications, although nobody expects them to be the definitive answer to forecasting problems. ANNs are currently implemented in such computer packages as MATLAB, SAS, and SPSS.

Support Vector Machines

Support vector machines (SVMs) are a new generation of learning networks based on the Vapnik–Chervonenkis theory of statistical learning.[58] The VC theory of statistical learning is complex, but despite the complexity of the theory behind them, SVMs are typically not more difficult to implement than neural networks. Moreover, Gunn, Brown, and Bossley (1997) reported that the performance of SVMs is generally superior to that of traditional neural networks.

Classification and Regression Trees

Trees are ubiquitous in AI because they implement a natural way of searching variables. In AI, trees are called "identification trees." Ross Quinlan (1979) built a well-known family of identification trees. As an AI procedure, identification trees work by applying a sequence of binary classification tests to a set of examples. In this way, the method constructs a tree that exactly classifies each example.

Trees can be constructed as hierarchical sets of rules. For example, ID3, the best known system of the ID family of trees developed by Quinlan, has been used to mine databases in areas ranging from credit assessment to medical diagnosis. Quinlan described the application of ID3 to a database of patients with hypothyroid diseases. The system produced rules from a simple type—"If the patient's TSH

---

[58]Developed from 1960 to 1990 by Vladimir Vapnik and Alexey Chervonenkis. See Vapnik (1995, 1998).

[thyroid stimulating hormone] level is less than 6.05 units, then the classification is negative"—to more complicated types.

The generalizability of a tree depends on when the tree is stopped, thus creating an approximate classification. As in every application of automatic learning, understanding where to stop the accuracy of in-sample analysis is the critical task.

Classification can be interpreted as a kind of discrete regression, insofar as it assigns a discrete classification value to each item. *Classification and regression trees* are the statistical counterpart of Quinlan's identification trees. Classification and regression trees work by splitting variables into two or more segments, such as return ≤ 3 percent, return >3 percent. The objective is to identify what combination of values of the independent variables corresponds to a given value of the dependent variable. Each item might be identified by both continuous variables and categorical variables (i.e., discrete variables that identify categories). For example, a group of companies could be identified by both continuous variables (e.g., financial ratios) and by categorical variables (e.g., industrial sector). By successive splitting, one can identify what financial ratios and sector identifier correspond to a given credit rating. At the end of the process, the result is an exhaustive classification. In short, standard regressions work only with continuous variables, but classification and regression trees accept as inputs a combination of different types of variables, including discrete variables.

Various classification tree programs have been developed.[59] One of the most useful in finance and banking is the CART® method.[60] For example, CART methods have been widely used to determine credit ratings and to detect credit card fraud. Our survey revealed that a number of asset management firms use CART methods in portfolio management (see Chapter 11). These firms consider the results satisfactory.

Genetic Algorithms

Genetic algorithms (GAs) are probabilistic optimizers. Given a function, GAs implement a systematic search for the maximum of that function by exploring the domain where the function is defined. The searching process is driven by the generation of random numbers. The search is not random; it is guided by genetic principles, in the sense that the mechanism of the search is inspired by genetic concepts.

GAs, which were inspired by genetic evolution in biology, were conceived by Holland (1976). According to the modern concept of evolution, random mutations produce individuals with new features. Those new features that make an individual

---

[59]Classification trees include the QUEST program of Loh and Shih (1997), C&RT devised by Breiman, Friedman, Olshen, and Stone (1984), FACT developed by Loh and Vanichestakul (1988), the THAID method of Morgan and Messenger (1973), and the CHAID approach of Kass (1980).
[60]CART is a registered trademark of California Statistical Software.

better adapted to the environment are preserved whereas other mutations disappear. Genetic evolution seems to be an efficient mechanism in terms of adaptation of various living beings to different environments.

Holland had the idea of creating a computational version of genetic evolution. Genetic computation proceeds in steps. The basic units for computation are arrays of zeros and ones called "chromosomes." The function to be optimized is defined on the chromosomes. At each step, random mutations are introduced in the chromosomes and operations that swap portions of the contents of chromosomes are applied. These operations mimic what happens in sexual reproduction. Those new chromosomes that correspond to higher values of the function to be maximized are retained.

In problem-solving applications, chromosomes represent possible solutions to the problem and the function to be optimized represents the objective. For example, in a trading application, chromosomes might represent trading strategy.

GAs can be considered optimizers or searching strategies. Ultimately, problem solving is implemented through an optimization process. One defines a space of variables to be searched, the variables that define the problem, and an objective function, called the "fitness function," that defines the quality of the solution. Problem solving consists of searching for the maximum of the objective function. GAs are useful in problem solving because, given their probabilistic nature, they do not get stuck in local maximum or minimum values, as often happens with conventional optimizers.

GAs have been used as a problem-solving paradigm. For example, Koza (1992) used genetic algorithms to implement genetic programming, a technique to develop computer programs automatically. In the domain of financial modeling, Leinweber used genetic algorithms to improve asset allocation strategies. He coded various models as chromosomes and defined a fitness function in terms of prediction results. The GAs explored a vast number of models and determined the optimal models. Results, reported in Kiernan (1994), were satisfactory.

A number of applications have been described in the finance literature. Armano, Marchesi, and Murru (2005) presented an application to forecasting stock indices. The forecasting activity results from the interaction of a population of "experts," each integrating genetic and neural technologies. An expert is a genetic classifier designed to control the activation of a feed-forward ANN. Applied to the S&P 500, this system exhibited remarkable forecasting performance.[61]

Thawornwong and Enke (2004) described the use of GAs for selecting predictors. The objective was to examine whether using recent relevant variables leads to additional improvements in stock return forecasting. The authors claimed that

---

[61]Many of these applications were designed as proprietary trading applications. As a consequence, only overall descriptions of the methods are available.

neural network models that use the recent relevant variables generated higher profits with lower risks than the buy-and-hold strategy, conventional linear regression, the random walk model, or neural network models that used constant relevant variables.

Text Mining

Text mining broadly defines a set of computer applications that can handle nonstructured data. Examples are reading, classifying, and summarizing text. It also includes automatic translation and the ability to search databases of textual data.

Text mining encompasses two technologies. The first is a body of technologies that handles text not specifically prepared for automatic processing. For example, an application might search a database of scientific articles and prepare abstracts of each paper. The second type of technology consists of handling texts that have already been conceived for automatic treatment. The *semantic web* is one such technology.

The first type of technology proved to have limited applications in finance. The reason is that texts now being produced, such as news and research reports, are prepared for automatic handling. The second type of technology is proving highly valuable. In connection with the diffusion of standards and with Web-searching technologies, the automatic handling of news and reports is now embedded in most information service providers.

Conclusion

The attractiveness of AI in financial modeling rests on three primary reasons:
- AI is not a black box but can deal with rules and statements that can be understood.
- AI can deal with a broad variety of categorical and continuous variables.
- AI can learn and solve problems that are only partially formulated.

The fact that AI is not a black box has proved to be less appealing than anticipated. Trees and rule-based systems are certainly not black boxes, and their working can be understood, but the number of rules that a large system can handle generally exceeds what human beings can effectively handle. In addition, growing familiarity with econometric modeling has reduced the demand for systems that can be followed. Our recent survey revealed that many people feel comfortable with black boxes.

AI's ability to learn to solve problems with both categorical and continuous variables is an important asset of AI methods. CART methods are often used because the modeler needs to use heterogeneous variables. Methods like CART, however, can be considered part of mainstream statistical analysis. CART does not contain much more artificial intelligence than does any other estimation technique.

The third point is the critical element that divides AI applications from conventional modeling. Unfortunately, the expectation that AI would allow problems to be solved automatically from incomplete or fuzzy data has proved to be unfounded. True, a well-trained pattern recognition application can recognize human faces or handwritten characters perhaps better than humans can, but those applications are well specified. The possibility of feeding computers data and news and letting the machines find profitable strategies is a far cry from reality. Although computers can perform repetitive operations at a speed that is billions of times that of human capabilities, the possibility of replacing intuition and judgment is remote. Problems need to be well defined and data well specified for AI to succeed. Ultimately, AI and machine learning are an extension of more conventional modeling that allow handling of broader sets of data.

7. Model Selection, Data Snooping, Overfitting, and Model Risk

Model selection is fraught with pitfalls—in particular, data snooping and over-fitting—but methods are available for mitigating these risks. Model selection is typically part of a process of innovation in methodologies in use at asset management firms. By the standards of modern science and technology, innovation in equity modeling is slow and difficult, for both technical and business reasons.

Finance has traditionally been associated with speculation and deal making. Since the broad diffusion of equity holdings after World War II in the United States and as of the 1990s in Western Europe, the management of equity portfolios has been entrusted to professionals whose knowledge and judgment are considered to enable them to produce returns in excess of what the investor might be able to obtain without professional assistance (for example, by stock selection or indexing). The ability of portfolio managers to realize excess returns has been questioned, however, by academic writers—starting with Samuelson (1965) and Fama (1965). These writers observed that financial markets are efficient. As a consequence, investment managers cannot produce excess returns; they can only optimize the risk–return trade-offs of investments.

Although studies showed that portfolio managers cannot consistently produce excess returns, the long bull market of the 1980s and 1990s made these discussions appear to be irrelevant: Investors were happy with the double-digit returns. The 1987 market crash forced some intellectual discipline into the equity investment process. Many firms introduced risk management to supervise the risk taking of asset managers and, in some cases, the risk position of the entire firm. Institutional investors were also instrumental in pushing asset management firms to adopt a more disciplined investment process.

The size and complexity of modern equity markets also played a role. The investable universe of traded stocks in the United States is presently several thousands.[62] No individual can have knowledge of a universe this size. Even if a

---

[62]The Russell 3000 Index represents about 99 percent of the variation in the U.S. equity market, and the Russell 1000 Index represents about 90 percent, but many of the smaller stocks are illiquid. What the "investable universe" is depends greatly on what kind of investment strategy a portfolio manager follows. The Wilshire 5000 Index contains about 5,000 stocks, and Wilshire considers all of them to be tradable to some degree.

firm employs specialized managers, the problem of understanding the correlations, cross-autocorrelations, and feedbacks (delayed response, momentum, reversal, and mean reversion/cointegration) among investments that have been empirically ascertained is not solvable without computerized models. For example, the S&P 500 Index contains approximately 125,000 pairwise correlations. These correlations are noisy and cannot be directly applied in portfolio management. By reducing the problem to correlations between a small number of factors (10–15 factors), factor analysis can reduce the number of correlations to 50–120. Without computers and statistical software, such an analysis is impossible. Adding cross-autocorrelations and feedbacks compounds the situation. As a consequence, modeling capabilities are necessary if an asset manager is to understand the markets and produce excess returns for clients.

Model Selection

In practice, model selection involves some interplay between business requirements and economic intuition. Business needs can be of various kinds, including the need to build or modify a suite of models and the need to model specific markets, market segments, or market regimes. Given a broad business need, the starting point of the modeler will be economic intuition; a purely data-mining approach in which the modeler probes data automatically in a search for patterns is not feasible (see Chapter 6). Even if the modeler decides to use machine-learning methods (see Chapter 6), some economic intuition to suggest a basic approach will be required. For example, intuition will suggest whether to use an *explanatory model*, which is based on exogenous factors, or an *autopredictive model*, which makes predictions on the basis of its own past.

Or the process may be the reverse: The economic intuition of the modeler may suggest a business opportunity. For example, a modeler might suggest examining specific market segments or specific patterns in financial markets that can be exploited. This process necessitates the sharing and managing of knowledge, something many asset management firms find difficult to foster.

Once the economic intuition has been articulated, the process of model selection can begin in earnest. The process consists of a sequence of four steps:
1. formulating the econometric hypothesis,
2. building the model,
3. estimating the model, and then,
4. testing the model.

Suppose, for example, that the objective is to model the economic intuition that a set of company financial ratios are good predictors of stock returns. The first step is to formulate the econometric hypothesis that embodies this intuition.

Among the decisions that have to be made are the choice of regressions (i.e., linear or nonlinear), the number and type of predictors, and the number of lags. Perhaps the modeler wants to use functions (modifications) of financial ratios, such as logarithms, or to extract special predictors formed as combinations of returns and/ or exogenous variables.

Next, the model has to be constructed as a software program, and its parameters must be estimated on sample data.

After estimation, the model must be tested. A number of tests can be performed on sample data. For example, in a linear regression, one can use sample data to test the relative importance of regressors. The real issue, however, is whether the model performs well when applied to new data—out-of-sample data. For this reason, the model has to be tested on test data that are different from the data used for estimating the model.

The construction process is only a general prescription, not a formal method-ology, for model building. Despite many efforts in problem solving, no "recipe" for model design exists.[63] Each step requires creative thinking. The testing and analysis of models, however, is a well-defined step-by-step methodology with a sound scientific foundation. The most important part of the discipline required in model selection is implementation of a rigorous testing methodology. We cover some of the standard testing procedures later in this chapter.

Simple vs. Complex Models

An important lesson in the theory of learning is that a key virtue for models is simplicity. Complex models require huge amounts of data for estimation and testing.

Trade-offs always have to be made among model complexity, explanatory power, and the size of available datasets. Despite their apparent superabundance, economic and financial data are actually scarce relative to what is needed to estimate many kinds of models. For example, the 125,000 individual possible pairwise correlations in the S&P 500 need to be reduced. Only a tiny fraction of the potential correlation structure is revealing; the rest is noise.

Financial econometrics ignores the details and attempts to determine *probabi-listic* laws. Discovering probabilistic laws with confidence, however, requires work-ing with large samples. The samples available for financial econometric analysis are too small to allow for a safe estimate of probability laws; small changes in the sample induce changes in the laws.

As a result of this scarcity of economic data, many different statistical models, even simple ones, can be compatible with the same data with roughly the same level of statistical confidence. Therefore, simplicity is a fundamental requirement. If two

---

[63]The same is true in almost all sectors of design and engineering.

models have roughly the same explanatory power, the simpler model—that is, the one with a smaller number of parameters to estimate—is preferable.

Machine-Learning Approach to Model Selection

The salient feature of machine learning, which is discussed at length in Chapter 6, is its universality. By its nature, machine learning can be adapted to any process. Machine learning—a by-product of the diffusion of computers—is characterized by the following:

- a set of empirical data that requires explanation,
- models that include an unbounded number of parameters,
- the ability of models to fit sample data with any desired degree of precision if the number of parameters is not constrained, and
- learning methodologies to constrain the number of parameters.

Neural networks, a machine-learning tool widely used to model data, illustrate how models can fit data with arbitrary precision. If one allows a sufficient number of layers and nodes, a neural network can approximate any given function with arbitrary precision.

The key concept of the theory of machine learning, however, is that a model that perfectly fits sample data has *no* explanatory power; that is, the model captures noise but does not capture any true feature of the data. The cause is the assumption that empirical data are described by some simple structure with a large amount of noise superimposed. In an economic context, machine learning can perfectly explain sample data, but if it does so, the explanation has no forecasting power because it fits noise. This phenomenon is called "overfitting."

To address the problem, the theory of machine learning constrains model complexity so that models fit sample data only partially but, in return, retain some forecasting power. Constraints typically embody a trade-off between the size of samples and the complexity of models. Fundamentally, large sample datasets support more complex models. If the sample dataset is small, the model can learn only simple patterns—provided that the patterns do indeed exist.

In most practical applications, the theory of machine learning works by introducing a *penalty function* to decide between various models. Adding parameters reduces the errors in sample but is penalized by the penalty function. Models can be compared by adding the penalty function to the *likelihood function* (see Chapter 9). The result is an ideal trade-off between model complexity and forecasting ability.

The theory of machine learning offers no guarantee of success: It is always possible to fit simple models to random patterns. To illustrate this point, we can generate a random walk and fit a polynomial of low order to the path. **Figure 7.1** illustrates how a polynomial of order 5 seems to capture some real behavior of data. But because the data are random, the fit is spurious.

Figure 7.1. Polynomial Fitting of a Random Walk with a Polynomial of Degree 5

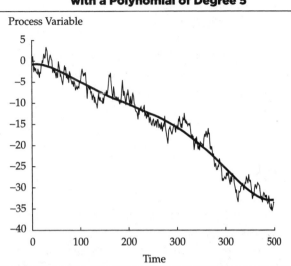

Finding Real Patterns

When analyzing a dataset made up of many patterns—for example, many time series of stock prices—one can always find patterns that look profitable in sample. For instance, in large sets, some patterns will seem to follow a profitable trend. A modeler who tries to find rare or unique patterns in large sets of data is erring because these patterns are typically not permanent and disappear in test data and in real data. This mistake is made easy by the availability of powerful computers that can explore large amounts of data. With the help of a computer, one can easily test the existence of interesting patterns in a large number of generated paths. To avoid looking for ephemeral patterns, one must stick rigorously to the paradigm of statistical tests. That is, one should not look for patterns that are exceptional but for patterns that appear with a *frequency* that allows rejecting the hypothesis that they are the product of chance.

Capturing the exceptional was an important source of failure in early data mining applications. Excited by the power of computers to discover hidden structures, many investigators failed to understand that in large databases, one can discover almost any structure. The development of the rigorous theory of machine learning shed light on exactly what structures can and cannot be learned.

The temptation to look for the exceptional is often difficult to recognize and resist. Suppose we are constructing a trading strategy based on a forecasting system that analyzes several hundred return processes. We may be tempted to base our trading strategy on selecting a small number of stocks that exhibit the highest returns. By doing so, however, we are likely to experience unpleasant surprises because many of the stocks selected will have been selected by chance. To reduce the risk of choosing spurious returns, we must select a large number of stocks. But choosing the optimal number of stocks to include in the strategy might not be a trivial task: It depends on the sampling distribution of returns (see Chapter 9 on estimation) and the amount of noise in the investable universe.

Note also that good practice calls for testing any model or pattern recognition method against a surrogate random sample generated with the same statistical characteristics as the empirical sample. For example, a model and strategy intended to find excess returns should be tested on a set of computer-generated random walks. If the proposed strategy finds profit in the computer-generated random walks, the strategy must be reconsidered.

Data Snooping

Calibrating models on some dataset, called the "training set," and testing them on another dataset, called the "test set," is good practice. Failure to do so is data snooping. Needless to say, the test set must be large and must cover all possible patterns, at least in some approximate sense. For example, to test a trading strategy, one needs to test data in many varied market conditions—those with high volatility and those with low volatility, in expansionary and recessionary periods, in various correlation situations, and so on.

Data snooping is not always easy to understand or detect. Suppose that a new model has not passed the tests and the modeling team starts the model selection process again. If the modelers use the same data for the new effort, some data snooping is unavoidable.

The real danger is the possibility that no true data-generation process (DGP) exists.[64] If so, through trial and error, the team may still hit upon a strategy that performs well in-sample but poorly when applied in the real world. Another form of hidden data snooping is when a methodology is finely calibrated to sample data. Again, a calibration parameterization may be found by trial and error that works well in the sample but poorly in the real world.

There is no sound theoretical way to avoid this problem *ex ante*. "Resampling" techniques have been proposed to alleviate the problem. Intuitively, the idea behind resampling is that a stable DGP calibrated on any portion of the data should work on the remaining data. Widely used resampling techniques include "leave-one-out" and "bootstrapping." The bootstrap technique creates surrogate data from the initial sample data.[65]

---

[64]The DGP of a series is a mathematical process that computes the future values of the variables given all information known at time t.

[65]The term "bootstrap" was given to this methodology because of initial skepticism about its soundness. It comes from the fictional Baron Munchausen, who lifted himself out of a well by pulling on his own bootstrap. Bootstrapping is an important technique but its description goes beyond the scope of this book. For a useful review of bootstrapping, see Davison and Hinkley (1999).

Survivor Bias

The sample data can also hold pitfalls. In addition to errors and missing data, one of the most common (and dangerous) problems with sample data is survivor bias. This bias is a consequence of selecting time series—in particular, asset price time series—by criteria that apply at the *end* of the period, not the beginning. For example, suppose a sample contains 10 years of price data for all stocks that are in a given index today and that existed for the previous 10 years. This sample is apparently well formed, but it is biased. In fact, the sample is made up of only the companies that have "survived" in sufficiently good shape to (still) be in the index. Those firms that were in the index in the period under investigation but are no longer there—because of bankruptcy, for example—have been ignored.

To illustrate the importance of survivor bias, we describe a simple experiment. We choose a large sample of price processes—the S&P 500 or the MSCI Europe Index over six or seven years. We implement a simple trading strategy that rebalances portfolios at regular intervals by buying or keeping the 20–30 highest priced stocks and selling short the corresponding 20–30 lowest priced stocks. In general, in the middle of this strategy's duration—from about the second to the fourth year—it will provide an exceptional return. The reason is that in the middle period, we find distressed companies that were nonetheless able to recover and remain in the index. Any trading strategy whose profits are low in the beginning and the end but high in-between should raise flags: The profits may be the result of survivor bias.

Avoiding survivor bias appears simple in principle: Base any sample selection on the stocks in the index at the beginning (rather than at the end) of the training period so that no invalid information enters the strategy prior to trading. The fact that companies are founded, closed, and merged, however, plays havoc with such a simple model. In fact, calibrating a simple model requires data on each asset for the entire training period—which, in itself, introduces a potentially large training bias. On the one hand, a simple model cannot handle processes that start or end in the middle of the training period. On the other hand, models that take into account the foundation or closing of companies are often not simple.

This problem has no easy solution. Care is required in estimating the possible performance biases consequent to sample biases. For example, suppose we use models today that were trained on the past three or four years of return data to make a forecast (using the same processes) of future returns. Clearly, data snooping is not involved because we used only information available prior to forecasting. But we must understand that we are estimating our models from data that contain biases. In other words, snooping and biases are not the same; a model that does not involve snooping can still contain biases and be unreliable (or even unusable) for forecasting.

Moving Windows and Regime Changes

So far, we have assumed that the DGP exists as a time-invariant model. Can we assume that the DGP varies, however, and that it can be estimated on a moving window? If so, how can the DGP be tested?

These complex questions do not have an easy answer. One aspect is whether we assume the processes change slowly or dramatically. Processes whose parameters change slowly are considered to be *evolutionary* processes. Processes that undergo singular changes at fixed or random time points are said to have "structural breaks" or "regime shifts." Do the economy and the markets experience evolutionary processes with slowly changing parameters, or do they experience structural breaks, or are both evolutionary processes and regime changes at work? If economic/market processes are evolutionary, modelers can hope to calibrate them on moving windows by slowly adapting parameters to changing situations. If the economy/market is subject to breaks or shifts, however, and if the time between breaks is long, models will perform well for a while and then, at the point of the break, degrade until a new model is learned.

Moreover, the economy and markets appear to experience *periodic* regime changes; they oscillate between different states. Obvious examples are the boom and bust cycles in the economy and bull and bear markets. In this case, if the regime changes are frequent and the interval between the changes short, one can use a model that incorporates the changes. The result is typically a nonlinear model, such as the Markov switching model (see Chapter 8). Estimating models of this type is onerous because of the nonlinearities inherent in the models and the long training periods required. An alternative is to try estimating models in various regimes, as long as the regimes are recognizable, and then use dynamically adjusted weights to calculate a weighted average of the model results. This approach is the idea behind *random coefficient models* (see Longford 1993).

Conclusion

To choose a modeling strategy, one must first keep in mind that if the model parameters change rapidly, the model coefficients are noisy and do not carry genuine information. Simply reestimating the model will not be sufficient, therefore, for finding model parameters that are useful for forecasting. One must determine how to separate noise from information in the coefficients. For example, a large vector autoregressive (VAR) model used to represent prices or returns will generally be unstable. To reestimate the model frequently would not make sense, so one should first reduce the model's dimensionality by, for example, factor analysis.

If the model parameters change slowly or, what is better, if a slow change is superimposed on the natural noise of the estimation process, one has to determine the nature of the change. Understanding if and how changes actually occur requires long time series. An analyst at a fairly large asset management firm who was interviewed for this monograph summarized the situation as follows: "In a couple thousand years, we will perhaps know how prices really behave." Structural breaks have received much attention in recent literature. Many tests have been suggested that allow detecting the presence of structural breaks, but given the size of available samples, the power of these tests is questionable.

Until we know more about how prices behave, we can use statistical tools to make educated guesses about the nature of price change. Modeling regime shifts is intrinsically more onerous than modeling simple linear processes. For this reason, the usual choice is to estimate models on a moving window—perhaps adding other techniques to reduce error, such as averaging the results of different models.

The length of the training window is clearly an issue. The need to calibrate the training window introduces the danger of data snooping. In fact, to make a meaningful calibration, one must see how models behave in the sample data and in the test (out-of-sample) data. In this situation (i.e., the joint consideration of the training data and the test data), data snooping is practically unavoidable. Again, no clear-cut theoretical solution exists. Modelers must use the available statistical test tools in addition to intuition and reasoning.

Clearly, simplicity (i.e., having only a small number of parameters to calibrate) is a virtue in financial modeling. A simple model that works well is to be favored over a complex model that runs the risk of producing unpredictable results. Nonlinear models, in particular, are always subject to the danger of unpredictable, chaotic behavior; extra care is required when they are used to avoid generating chaotic behavior. Every step of the discovery process has to be checked for empirical, theoretical, and logical consistency.

8. Predictive Models of Return

In the less rewarding markets that have followed the 2000 U.S. market downturn, the need of asset management firms to reduce costs and improve performance was behind the search for models with predictive capability. Predictive return models make conditional forecasts of expected returns that are dependent on the present information set. The use of these models represents a departure from the past, in that finance theory had held that expected returns are *unpredictable*.

A number of econometric models are currently being used in equity portfolio management to model risk and returns in a predictive environment. In this chapter, we explore four major families of predictive return models:
- regressive models that regress returns on factors (or predictors),
- linear autoregressive models that regress returns on their own lagged values,
- dynamic factor models and cointegration-based models that mix prices and returns, and
- hidden-variable models that try to capture regime change.[66]

Generally, when analysts consider adopting a model, they first need to ask a number of questions. The most important questions are the following:
- What are the statistical properties of the model?
- How many variables should enter the model?
- How does one estimate the model?
- How does one test whether the model is correct?
- How can the consequences of errors in the choice of model be mitigated?

The focus of this chapter is on the first question—that is, the statistical properties of various families of models. We discuss the basic statistical concepts behind models and their economic meaning, but we omit most mathematical details.

An important factor in the growing adoption of modeling is the availability of software packages that implement the principal econometric building blocks. Most of the models described in this chapter can be implemented with minimal coding by using functions available in standard statistical software packages.[67]

---

[66] In addition to these models, analysts have developed models based on machine learning, but because such models are based on different principles from those of a more classical econometric approach, we discuss them separately in Chapter 6.

[67] Software is available from such companies as E-ViEWS, GAUSS, MATLAB, PcGive, and SAS.

Regressive Models

Regressive models of returns are generally based on linear regressions on "factors" (which are also referred to as "predictors"). Linear regressions are simple yet powerful statistical models. Conceptually, regressive models may be categorized as one of two fundamental kinds:

- *Static* regressive models do not make predictions about the future. These models regress present returns on present factors.
- *Predictive* regressive models regress *future* returns on present and past factors to make predictions.

Although the mathematical principles of linear regression are the same for both categories, the economic meanings are significantly different.

Principles of Linear Regression.[68] Regression is a statistical construct for expressing the notion of *dependence* between random variables. Consider the simplest case: Assume we have two random variables, X and Y.[69] If X and Y are deterministic variables, we say that one variable—say, Y—depends on the other variable—in this case, X—*if* there is a functional dependence of the sort that if the value of X is known, the value of Y is also known with certainty. In a statistical environment, this concept of dependence is too strict and, instead, dependence is expressed through the concepts of *conditional distribution* and *conditional expectation*. Thus, we say that random variable Y depends on variable X if the distribution of Y depends on the value assumed by X.[70]

It is necessary to distinguish between two types of dependence of Y on X:

- First, the distribution of variable Y depends on variable X, and the expected value of Y depends on X.

---

[68] For a more detailed review of linear regressions, see Chapter 9 in DeFusco, McLeavey, Pinto, and Runkle (2004).

[69] A random variable is a variable that can assume one of many values, subject to uncertainty. The defining property of a random variable is that for any two values a and b, one can assign a probability to the event that the variable x is greater than a and smaller than b. Thus, by referring to a variable as random, we do not mean that it is a random walk or unpredictable.

[70] The concepts of conditional distribution and conditional expectation are subject to many important mathematical subtleties. The main reason is that the probability of a single value of a variable is zero. Thus, in conditioning, one cannot divide for the probability of the conditioning variable, as we do in the usual formula $P(A|B) = P(AB)/P(B)$ that defines the conditional probability of event A given event B. It may be helpful to think of conditioning as a parameterization of the distribution—that is, the distribution of Y is parameterized with X. But although this approach may help intuition, it hides fundamental probabilistic facts about conditioning—such as the factorization of the joint density of X,Y into a conditional density and a marginal density. Interested readers can consult Focardi and Fabozzi (2004) or any advanced text on probability.

- Second, the distribution of variable Y depends on variable X, but the expected value of Y *does not* depend on X.[71]

In the second case, the dependence includes only the variance and higher moments, not the expectation.

Now, suppose that the expectation of Y depends on the value assumed by X. The regression function of Y on X is the deterministic function that expresses the expectation of Y conditional on the value assumed by the variable X. Linear regressions are characterized by a *linear regression function*—for example:

$$Y = aX + b + \varepsilon,$$

where a is the coefficient of regression of Y on X, b is the intercept or constant term, and ε is a zero-mean noise term.

Two important observations are in order:

- First, the concept of regression does not imply any notion of time. Analysts can regress one time series on another time series, however, in the sense that a sequence of regressions is carried out by performing one at each time step. Because most regressions are of one time series on another and the results are usually thought of as meaningful in an intertemporal time context, the fact that there is no dependency on time must be checked. As shown in Chapter 9 on estimation, this operation may result in correlations between the noise terms—which has significant consequences for the estimation process.

- Second, the dependent variable can be regarded as either a deterministic variable or a random variable. If it is regarded as a deterministic variable, which is conceptually the simpler case, the regression equation is considered to be a parameterization of the distribution of the dependent variables not subject to uncertainty. If it is regarded as a random variable (in which case, both variables are random variables), the modeler can introduce probabilistic and statistical concepts, such as the correlation coefficient of Y, X.

Linear regressions are simple statistical models. The conditional distribution of returns is always the same as that of the error term; that is, if the error term is normally distributed, the returns are also normally distributed, and if the error term is not normally distributed, then neither is the conditional distribution of returns. However, the unconditional distribution of returns depends on the distributions of both the factors and the error terms. Linear regressions can also be determined if the noise terms and the factors exhibit infinite variance (see Rachev and Mittnik 2000).

---

[71]This restricted type of dependence is important in financial econometrics. In fact, returns, after appropriate discounting, are believed to be martingales—that is, processes in which the expectation of returns does not depend on past values of returns but in which higher moments may be dependent on present and past returns.

The quality of a linear regressive model (i.e., its ability to explain data) can be measured by evaluating the ratio of the variance explained by the model to the total variance or, alternatively, the ratio of the variance of the noise terms to the total variance. The total variance is the variance of the dependent variable (i.e., the returns). The variance explained by the regressive model is the total variance minus the error variance. This measure is the *coefficient of determination* and is commonly denoted by R^2.

A critical issue in regression analysis is the number of factors. In principle, if the number of factors with some predictive power is increased, the quality of the regression should improve. As explained in Chapter 9, however, increasing the number of factors increases the noise in the estimates, thereby reducing forecasting accuracy. As a result, modelers face a trade-off between the number of factors and accuracy: Indiscriminately adding predictive factors reduces the accuracy of predictions.

Static Regressive Models of Return. The best known example of a static regressive model of return is the capital asset pricing model (CAPM). Suppose the risk-free return is r_f and the return of the market portfolio is r_M. The CAPM states that each stock return, r_i, is characterized by a constant beta, β, such that the expected excess return of that stock (i.e., the difference between the return of that stock and the risk-free return) is proportional to the expected market excess return. Proportionality constant β is the covariance between the stock and the market portfolio scaled (i.e., divided) by the variance of the market portfolio and is a measure of the stock's systematic risk.

The CAPM can also be expressed as a static linear regression in which each stock's excess return is regressed on the market excess return plus a noise term. Static *multifactor* models can also be expressed as linear regressions. For example, the arbitrage pricing theory (APT) model is a linear regression of each stock's return on a small number of factors. In general, these factors can be interpreted as portfolios.

Figure 8.1 illustrates the effects of a CAPM-type regression on price processes. In it, the market process is simulated by the MSCI Europe Index for the period January 1999 through April 2005. Beta represents risk: Higher beta should command a higher expected return. The higher beta stock has a negative excess return when market returns are positive and a positive excess return when market returns are negative. The lower beta stock behaves in the opposite way. Over the entire period, because the market return was negative, the higher beta stock exhibits a negative excess return and the lower beta stock exhibits a positive excess return.

Graphically in Figure 8.1, the price process of a stock with a beta greater than 1 seems to magnify the market fluctuations whereas the price process of a stock with a beta less than 1 seems to smooth market fluctuations. In both cases a constant drift with respect to the market appears.

Figure 8.1. Behavior of Stock Price Processes that Behave According to the CAPM, January 1999–April 2005

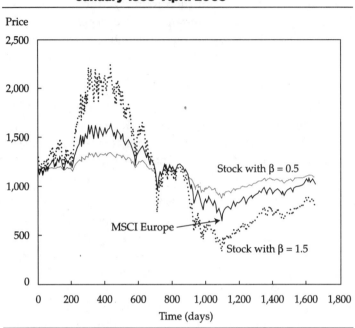

These regressions should be viewed as timeless relationships that are valid at any moment. They are *not* predictive because there is no time lag between the return and the factor. For example, in the CAPM, the conditional expectation of each stock's return at time *t* is proportional to the excess return of the market portfolio, which is not known at time *t*. Predictions would be possible only if one could predict the excess return of the market portfolio. If one wants to use the CAPM or APT to build a portfolio or to compute portfolio risk measures such as value at risk, some assumption about how to forecast the factor(s) is needed. The usual assumption is that the factors (and thus the returns) are sequences of independent and identically distributed random variables.

Note that nothing in the CAPM regression precludes assuming that the market portfolio return can be predicted. Should the market portfolio return be predictable, however, the theoretical static CAPM relationship would have to be replaced by a dynamic model because prices would be explosive if betas did not change. Theoretical dynamic asset-pricing models have been developed, but they have limited practical applicability, as explained in Chapter 7. In practice, for portfolio management, one needs simple models that can be estimated from the limited amount of empirical data. Note, however, that dynamic models, in which both expected returns and risk are predictable, do *not* contradict the basic principles of absence of arbitrage and market efficiency.

Predictive Regressive Models. The other family of regressive models of returns—the predictive regressive models—have been developed in the quest for models that predict returns. Consider a stock return, r_t, and a number of predictors—for example, a number of company financial ratios, $f_{i,t}$. A predictive linear regressive model assumes that the stock return at any given time t is a weighted average of its predictors at an earlier time plus a constant and some error.

Figure 8.2 illustrates the behavior of a predictive regression. The setting is the same as the CAPM but with a time lag; that is, the expected excess return of a stock at time t is beta times the excess return of the market at an earlier date. For illustration purposes, we chose a time lag of 50 days (that is, the stock price process begins 50 days after the market price process). Note that the path of the stock price has the same shape as that of the market but is shifted in time.

Figure 8.2. Predictive Regression

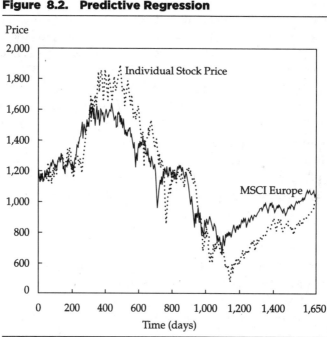

Predictive regressions can also be defined by regressing returns on factors at different lags. Models of this type are called *distributed lag* (DL) models. The advantage of these models is their ability to capture the eventual dependence of returns not only on factors but also on the *rate of change* of factors. To appreciate the economic importance of DL models, suppose we want to create a predictive model based on, among other factors, "market sentiment." Market sentiment is typically measured as a weighted average of analysts' forecasts. A reasonable assumption is that stock returns will be sensitive to the value of market sentiment but will be even more sensitive to *changes in* market sentiment. Hence, DL models will be useful in this setting.

Linear Autoregressive Models

In a linear autoregressive model, a variable is regressed on its own lagged values—that is, on its own past. If the model involves only one variable, it is called an "autoregressive" (AR) model. If more than one variable is regressed contemporaneously in the model, it is called a "vector autoregressive" (VAR) model because the model variables are now vectors (i.e., arrays of variables).[72]

An AR model prescribes that the value of a variable at time t be a weighted average of the values of the same variable at times $t-1, t-2, \ldots$, and so on (depending on number of lags) plus an error term. The weighting coefficients are the model parameters. If the model includes p lags, then p parameters must be estimated.

Now, consider a VAR model that includes two variables. The model expresses each variable as a weighted average of its own lagged values plus the lagged values of the other variable. If the model includes p lags, each variable is regressed on $2p$ lagged values, and therefore, the model includes $4p$ parameters. This reasoning can be extended to any number of variables. If the model includes n variables and p lags, each equation includes np lagged values. Because the model has n variables (and thus n equations), it has $n^2 p$ parameters. Note that no symmetry considerations can reduce the number of these parameters.

A VAR model with p lags is written as a VAR(p) model. As we are about to explain, every VAR(p) model is equivalent to a specific VAR(1) model. The equivalence is established by formally adding new variables that are the lagged values of other variables. In this way, a VAR(p) model with n equations is equivalent to a VAR(1) model with np equations.

Clearly, a VAR model can capture cross-autocorrelations; that is, a VAR model can model how values of a variable at time t are linked to the values of another variable at some other time. An important question is whether these links are causal or simply correlations.[73]

These considerations make clear that a VAR model can model only a small number of series. A large number of series—for example, the return processes for the individual securities making up such aggregates as the S&P 500 Index—would result in a huge number of parameters to estimate. For example, if one wanted to model the daily returns of the S&P 500 with a VAR model that included two lags, the number of parameters to estimate would be $500 \times 500 \times 2 = 500{,}000$ parameters.

---

[72]We focus on VAR models because the properties of AR models are similar to, although simpler than, those of VAR models.

[73]For a discussion of the analysis of causality in VAR models, see Fabozzi, Focardi, and Kolm (2006a).

To have at least as many data points as parameters, one would need at least four years of data, or 1,000 trading days, for each stock return process, which is 1,000 × 500 = 500,000 data points. Under these conditions, estimates would be extremely noisy and the estimated model, meaningless.

We explain later how dynamic factor analysis can significantly reduce the number of parameters to estimate. Unrestricted VAR models remain a key building block of any dynamic factor modeling; however, in this case, they model common factors.[74] In addition, unrestricted VAR models can be used to model the behavior of indices and broad aggregates.

Statistical Properties of Autoregressive Models. Autoregressive models are truly dynamic models, in the sense that they describe the evolution of a system starting from initial conditions. Suppose we create a VAR model to represent the returns of a number of indices. Using a computer, we can run a simulation in which we, step by step, update the model equations from initial conditions. In fact, a VAR model implements a data-generation process (DGP), which is a mechanism that is able to generate data with given statistical properties.

VAR models are of two basic types—stable and unstable. Stable VAR models generate stationary processes; unstable VAR models generate processes that can be explosive or integrated.

   Stable VAR models. Perhaps the easiest way to understand the statistical properties of a stable VAR model is by looking at the explicit form of its solutions. Consider a stable VAR process that starts from deterministic initial conditions and is subject to a stream of external shocks. This process describes what would happen in a computer simulation. The computer would start from some initial conditions and generate a random noise term at each step. In economic terms, the random noise terms can represent such phenomena as news or fluctuations in cash flows.

The response of a stable VAR model to each shock is an exponential with exponent less than 1. The solutions of a stable VAR model are thus sums of weighted exponentials with exponents less than 1, corresponding to past shocks. In all cases, the solutions decrease exponentially. As a consequence, the influence of the initial conditions dies out exponentially (i.e., the influence is damped) and becomes negligible. The influence of each random term will also die out exponentially.

Therefore, the solutions produced by a VAR model will, in every moment, be the sum of all past noise terms but exponentially damped. Consequently, only the most recent shocks will have a nonnegligible effect; the effects of initial conditions and of shocks in the distant past will vanish.

---

[74] A VAR model is called "unrestricted" if its parameters are allowed to assume any real value. A VAR model is called "restricted" if its coefficients can assume values only within a given range.

Figure 8.3 illustrates the behavior of stable solutions of VAR processes. We can thus imagine the solutions of a stable VAR process as stationary time series around some mean. These series will be subject to continuous mutual influences but will remain stationary. As Figure 8.3 shows, some of the solutions will exhibit oscillatory behavior while other solutions simply exhibit exponential decay. In all cases, solutions will exhibit autocorrelation; in other words, there will be a nonnegligible correlation between the values of each series at different time lags. Correlations will decay with time and eventually disappear.

Figure 8.3. VAR Processes with Various Solutions

A. VAR Processes with Oscillating and Exponentially Growing Solutions

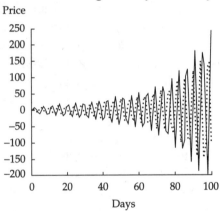

B. VAR Processes with Oscillating and Exponentially Damped Solutions

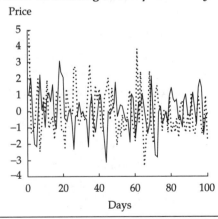

(continued)

Figure 8.3. VAR Processes with Various Solutions (continued)

C. VAR Processes with Integrated Solutions

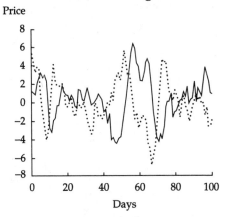

Price

D. VAR Processes with Exponentially Damped Solutions

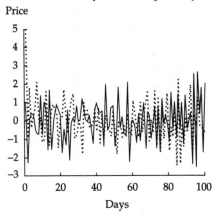

Price

The behavior of the autocorrelation function is quite intuitive. Clearly, at each moment, the future of the system is determined partially by the deterministic response to the present and past shocks and partially by new shocks. The portion of future behavior that depends on the response to present and past shocks is responsible for correlations. As this predictable part decays with time, the entire autocorrelation function will decay. **Figure 8.4** shows the behavior of the autocorrelation function of a VAR(2) process. The dotted horizontal lines represent the confidence band; points within the band are not significant. The economic meaning is that the effects of present events and events in the immediate past will be felt for some time and only gradually become negligible and be replaced by new events.

Figure 8.4. Sample Autocorrelation Functions

A. VAR Process

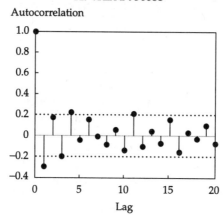

B. VAR Process

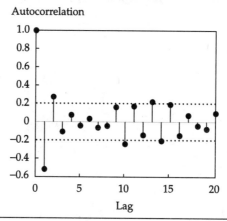

■ *Unstable VAR models.* All solutions of VAR models are exponentials. Unstable solutions of VAR models are exponentials with an exponent greater than or equal to 1. In this discussion, we exclude solutions with exponents greater than 1 because these solutions are explosive and thus economically irrelevant.

Solutions with exponent 1 originate *integrated processes*—that is, processes in which shocks accumulate and never decay. In many integrated processes, the error terms are autocorrelated. The simplest, but by no means only, example of an integrated process is a random walk. Integrated processes are processes in which a stationary process keeps on cumulating. In fact, by differencing an integrated process, one obtains a stationary process. **Figure 8.5** shows four paths of integrated processes. The pale solid line and the dashed line are autocorrelated.

Figure 8.5. Four Integrated Processes

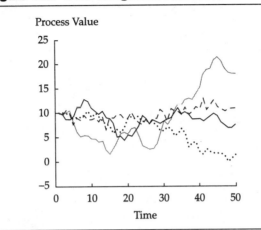

Suppose that an unstable VAR model has only integrated solutions and these solutions represent the logarithms of stock prices. These solutions can exhibit two fundamentally different types of behavior. The first alternative is that every possible portfolio formed with these stocks exhibits integrated behavior. The other, more interesting alternative is that although all solutions are individually integrated, linear combinations of (that is, portfolios formed with) these solutions may be stationary. This behavior is called "cointegration." It was first discovered in the 1980s by Robert Engle and Clive Granger (1987) and was among the reasons they received the Nobel Memorial Prize in Economic Sciences in 2003.

Given n integrated processes, there can be from 1 to $n - 1$ cointegrating relationships (i.e., different linear combinations that are stationary). If there are k cointegrating relationships, a crucial finding of Engle and Granger is that, then, there are $n - k$ common trends such that every other solution can be expressed as a linear regression on these common trends. **Figure 8.6** shows three cointegrated processes with two common trends.

Cointegration can be interpreted in various ways. We have already mentioned two potential implications: (1) the existence of stationary linear combinations and (2) the existence of common trends. A third important potential implication of cointegration is that *meaningful* linear regressions between integrated time series are possible. In general, a meaningful linear regression of one integrated time series on another integrated time series is not possible because they are both random. Such regressions are spurious, although they might well pass the R^2 test. If the series are cointegrated, however, the linear regressions are meaningful.

The problem of spurious regressions is one of the major difficulties in performing predictive regressions. We have discussed how financial ratios and other variables can be used as predictors of returns, but financial ratios are often close to

Figure 8.6. Three Cointegrated Processes with Two Common Trends

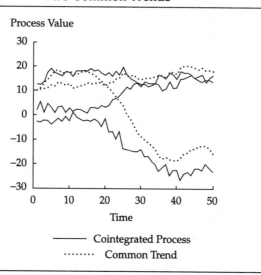

integrated processes. Therefore, regressing returns that are stationary variables on financial ratios may yield spurious predictive relationships.

Dynamic Factor Models

We previously discussed predictive regressive models, in which returns are linearly regressed on factors but the factors are left unmodeled. We described two types of regressive behavior—predictive and nonpredictive. In general, a model in which factors follow a VAR model and returns (or prices) are linearly regressed on these factors is a *dynamic factor model.*

Dynamic factor models are cointegrated models in which factors are the common trends. **Figure 8.7** uses three processes with a dynamic factor to illustrate the behavior of dynamic factor models.

Other formulations of dynamic factor models, however, are possible. In particular, dynamic factor models are a compact formulation of some *state-space model.* A state-space model is formed from two parts: the observable variables and the hidden state variables. State variables are auxiliary variables; they are not observable but are useful for describing the entire system. The dynamics of the state variables are modeled by a VAR(1) model; the dynamics of the observables are linear regressions of the observables on the state variables. Any VAR model and any dynamic factor model can be expanded into a state-space model.

In principle, the number of state variables can exceed the number of observables. For example, to prove the equivalence of a VAR(p) model to a state-space model, one has to expand the observables into a bigger number of state variables. In financial

Figure 8.7.   Three Processes with One Dynamic Factor

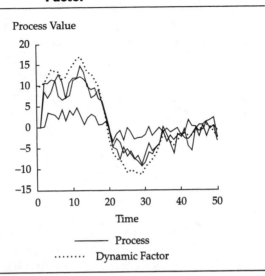

Process Value

Time

——— Process

········ Dynamic Factor

econometrics, however, the interest in state-space models and dynamic factor models arises from the possibility of *reducing* the model's dimensionality.

Recall that for a model to be useful, the number of parameters to be estimated needs to be small. A dynamic factor model fulfills this requirement by concentrating the dynamics of an aggregate (such as the S&P 500) into a small number of dynamic factors that, in turn, correspond to a small number of state variables. For example, a modeler might identify in the S&P 500 three dynamic factors modeled by a VAR with, say, four lags, which results in only 12 state variables rather than the initial 500.

Both dynamic factor models and state-space models can represent either integrated or stable processes. In the case of stable processes, the identification of factors with common trends is no longer valid because all processes are stationary.

In light of the equivalence of dynamic factor models with state-space models and, therefore, with VAR models, solutions to the two types of model have the same form already encountered—that is, sums of exponentials. From an economic perspective, the possibility of writing dynamic factor models of prices implies that returns are predictable. Note that VAR models or factor models of returns also imply that returns are predictable. But the ability to mix levels (i.e., prices) and differences (i.e., returns) in the same model adds significant forecasting possibilities. To see this point, suppose that we identified only one common trend for prices; that is, all prices are mean reverting on a single common trend. Behavior of this type cannot be generated by return processes with a finite memory.

Hidden-Variable Models

The state-space models are hidden-variable models in the sense that the state variables are not directly observable. State-space models are linear models, so one can use the same mathematical form of linear state-space models to represent a nonlinear family of hidden-variable models in which state variables represent the model parameters. Probably the best known of these processes is the *autoregressive conditional heteroscedasticity* (ARCH) and *generalized autoregressive conditional heteroscedasticity* (GARCH) family. ARCH/GARCH models use an autoregressive process to model the volatility of another process. The result is a rich representation of the behavior of the model volatility.

Another category of nonlinear hidden-variable models is the *Markov switching–vector autoregressive* (MS–VAR) family. These models do allow forecasting of expected returns. The simplest MS–VAR model is the Hamilton model (Hamilton 1989). In economics, this model is based on two random walk models—one with a drift for periods of economic expansion and the other with a smaller drift for periods of economic recession. The switch between the two models is governed by a probability transition table that prescribes the probability of switching from recession to expansion, and vice versa, and the probability of remaining in the same state.

The Hamilton model can be generalized to cover the case in which a probability transition table governs the switch to/from one of a set of VAR models. Such models implement regime switching.

Why Dynamic Models?

The salient characteristic of dynamic models of stock returns and stock prices is their ability to predict expected returns on the basis of the present and past values of the same returns plus—if greater model complexity is acceptable—other variables. Empirical studies have shown that returns exhibit some predictability. Indeed, returns and risk (e.g., variance) are somewhat predictable. The more difficult questions are whether and how return predictability can be turned into a profit. Any application of dynamic models in actual asset management must make sure that the risk–return trade-off remains positive.

9. Model Estimation

In this discussion of methodologies for estimating models, we introduce the concept of estimation and the concept of sampling distributions. We then discuss how estimation methods are applied to specific models.

Statistical Estimation and Testing

Most statistical models have parameters that must be estimated. Statistical estimation is a set of criteria and methodologies for determining the best estimates of parameters. Testing is complementary to estimation. Critical parameters are often tested before the estimation process starts in earnest, although some tests of the adequacy of models can be performed after estimation.

In general terms, statistics is a way to make inferences from a sample to the entire population from which the sample is taken. In financial econometrics, the sample is typically an empirical time series. Data may be returns, prices, rates, company-specific financial data, or macroeconomic data. The objective of estimation techniques is to estimate the parameters of models that describe the empirical data.

The key concept in estimation is that of *estimators*. An estimator is a function of sample data whose value is close to the true value of a parameter in a distribution. For example, the empirical average (i.e., the sum of the samples divided by the number of samples) is an estimator of the mean; that is, it is a function of the empirical data that approximates the true mean. Estimators can be simple algebraic expressions; they can also be the result of complex calculations.

Estimators must satisfy a number of properties. In particular, estimators

- should get progressively closer to the true value of the parameter to be estimated as the sample size becomes larger,
- should not carry any systematic error, and
- should approach the true values of the parameter to be estimated as rapidly as possible.

Being a function of sample data, an estimator is a random (i.e., stochastic) variable. Therefore, the estimator has a probability distribution referred to as the *sampling distribution*. In general, the probability distribution of an estimator is difficult to compute accurately from small samples but is simpler for large samples.

To illustrate these principles, we computer-generated 2 million random numbers extracted from a normal distribution with mean of 0 and variance of 1. We then computed the variance on 100,000 samples of 20 numbers, each selected from the given population. As shown in **Figure 9.1**, the sampling distribution is not normal. When we repeated the same calculations on samples of 100 sample points each, however, the sampling distribution became much closer to normal, as shown in **Figure 9.2**.

Figure 9.1. Sampling Distribution of the Mean and Variance for Samples of 20 Elements Each

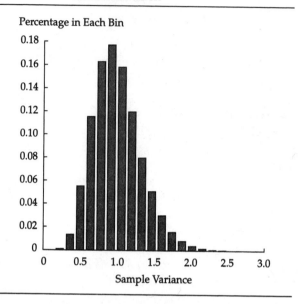

Figure 9.2. Sampling Distribution of the Mean and Variance for Samples of 100 Elements Each

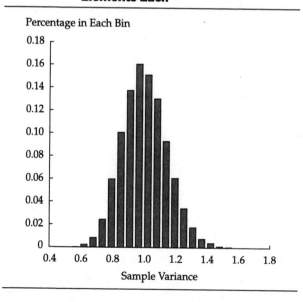

The sampling distribution is important because certain decisions, such as determining whether a process is integrated, must often be made on the basis of estimators. Because estimators are random variables, decisions are based on comparing empirical estimators with *critical values* computed from the sampling distribution. A critical value is a number that allows one to discriminate between accepting or rejecting a hypothesis. For example, suppose we need to know whether a process is integrated. Integration means that the autoregression parameter is 1. Even if a process is integrated, however, every estimate will give results different from 1 because of purely statistical fluctuations. But sampling theory of regressions allows us to determine critical values so that we can reject the hypothesis that the process is integrated if the autoregression coefficient is smaller or larger than the upper/lower critical values.[75]

Estimation Methods

Because estimation methods involve criteria that cannot be justified by themselves, they are subject to some arbitrariness. The crucial point is that, whereas an estimation process must "fit" a distribution to empirical data, any distribution can, with a few restrictions, be fitted to any empirical data. The choice of distributions thus includes an element of arbitrariness. Suppose we want to determine the probability distribution of the faces of a tossed coin, and in 1,000 experiments, heads comes out 950 times. We probably would conclude that the coin is highly biased and that heads has a 95 percent probability of coming up. We have no objective way, however, to rule out the possibility that the coin is fair and that we are experiencing an unlikely event. Ultimately, whatever conclusion we draw is arbitrary.

Three estimation methods are commonly used in financial econometrics: the least-squares, maximum-likelihood, and Bayesian methods.[76]

The Least-Squares Estimation Method. The least-squares (LS) estimation method is a best-fit technique adapted to a statistical environment. Suppose a set of points is given and we want to find the straight line that best approximates these points. In financial modeling, a point may represent, for example, a return at a given time. A sensible criterion in this case is to compute the distance of each point from a generic straight line, form the sum of the squares of these distances, and choose the line that minimizes this sum—in short, the ordinary least-squares (OLS) method.

---

[75]Critical values of the autoregressive parameters are tabulated and are available in all major time-series software packages.

[76]Other estimation methods include the M-methods, which are generalizations of the maximum-likelihood method; the method of moments, which estimates parameters as functions of the empirical moments; the instrumental variables method, which estimates a model parameter with the aid of additional "instrumental" variables; and the generalized method of moments, which is a generalization of the linear instrumental variables approach.

The least-squares method can be adapted to any set of points and to different functional forms (straight lines, polynomial functions, and so on). It can be used, for example, to regress the returns of a stock on a financial ratio.

The Maximum-Likelihood Estimation Method. The maximum-likelihood (ML) estimation method involves maximizing the likelihood of the sample given an assumption of the underlying distribution (for example, that it is a normal distribution or a uniform distribution). *Likelihood* is the distribution computed for the sample. For example, suppose a coin is biased so that heads has a 30 percent probability of coming up and tails, a 70 percent probability. What is the likelihood in a random independent sample of 3 heads and 2 tails coming up? It is $0.3 \times 0.3 \times 0.3 \times 0.7 \times 0.7$. The ML method would choose these parameters because they maximize the probability (likelihood) of the sample being observed.

As just noted, the ML method implies that one knows the form of the distribution; otherwise, one cannot compute the likelihood. ML methods can be used, for example, to estimate the long-run relationships (cointegration) between various rates of return.

Bayesian Estimation Methods. Bayesian estimation methods are based on an interpretation of statistics that is different from that of the OLS or ML methods. Bayesian statistics explicitly assume a *subjective* element in probability. This subjective element is expressed by the so-called *prior distribution*, which is the distribution that represents all available knowledge prior to data collection. Bayesian statistics use a specific rule, *Bayes' theorem*, to update prior probabilities as a function of the arrival of new data to form *posterior distributions*. Bayes' theorem simply states that the posterior distribution is the prior distribution multiplied by the likelihood. Thus, Bayesian estimates have three ingredients: a prior distribution, a likelihood, and an updating rule.

Note that to write the likelihood, one needs to know the form of the distribution—for example, that it is a Gaussian distribution. The prior distribution will typically be expressed as a distribution of the parameters of the likelihood.

In practice, the Bayesian estimate of a model implies that one has an idea of a typical model and that the estimated model is a "perturbation" of the typical model. Bayesian methods are frequently used to allow a portfolio manager to plug his or her own views into a model—that is, to subjectively influence or "perturb" the model.

Robust Estimation. With the widespread use of large predictive models having many parameters, the techniques of robust estimation (that is, estimation that is relatively insensitive to (1) a violation of one or more assumptions and/or (2) estimation errors in the inputs) have gained importance; they are now a key component of estimation technology. For example, robust estimation takes the uncertainty in the estimates into account in portfolio optimization (see Chapter 3).

The motivation for robust estimation is that, because of the size of available samples, estimates are typically noisy when large models are being estimated. In addition, data may contain mistakes. Therefore, extracting the maximum amount of meaningful information from a noisy process is important.

To understand the need for robust estimation, consider the estimation of a correlation matrix. The correlation between two random variables is a number that assumes values between –1 and ⌐1. The value 0 indicates absence of correlation. As discussed in the previous section, the empirical estimator of the correlation parameter is a random variable. Consider two normally distributed variables that are independent (consequently, the true, or population, correlation is zero). For n samples of these variables, it is known in statistics that the correlation parameter will, with 99 percent probability (99 percent of the time), be in the range of plus/minus three times the reciprocal of the square root of the number of samples. If we have 1,000 samples, the correlation parameter will fall (approximately) in the range between –0.1 and +0.1, with 99 percent probability. That is, with 1,000 samples, if the absolute value of their estimated correlation exceeds 0.1, we can conclude at a 99 percent confidence level that the two variables are correlated.

Now, consider the correlations of stock returns in a sample of 1,000 trading days (that is, four years) of an aggregate stock index. In the case of the S&P 500 Index, because of symmetry, the correlation matrix has approximately 125,000 entries. Returns on individual stocks are known to be strongly correlated with one another.[77] In fact, in any four-year period, the empirical average correlation well exceeds the 10 percent level. If we try to evaluate individual correlations (i.e., to discriminate between the correlation levels of various pairs), however, we glean little information. In fact, the distribution of empirical correlation coefficients in the entire correlation matrix is similar to random fluctuations around some mean correlation. If we were to feed this correlation matrix to a mean–variance optimizer, we would obtain meaningless (and dangerous) results—the so-called corner portfolios—because the optimizer would treat low or negative correlations appearing essentially at random, as though they represented actual investment opportunities.[78]

Separating information from noise is a difficult problem. For example, in the case of a correlation matrix, we have to extract a meaningful correlation structure from a correlation matrix whose entries are corrupted by noise. The problem of separating a signal (useful information) from noise by maximizing the "signal-to-noise ratio" is well known in engineering. Communications technology and speech and image recognition, to name a few, are areas where the minimization of noise is

---

[77]If stock returns were not correlated, diversification would make large portfolios nearly deterministic.
[78]In general, and all other things being equal, the lower the correlation a security has with other securities, the more desirable it is.

a critical component.[79] The following sections outline the techniques of robust estimation used for each class of financial models.

Estimation of Matrices

Consider the task of estimating a variance–covariance matrix. Suppose we have two random variables. Assume first that they have zero means. The variance of the two variables is defined as the expectation of their square, and the covariance, as the expectation of their product; the correlation is covariance scaled by dividing it by the square root of the individual variances (i.e., the volatilities). Suppose we have a *sample* formed by extracting n pairs of the two variables from a *population*. In this case, the empirical variance of each variable is the sum of the squares of the samples divided by the number of samples (i.e., the empirical average of the square of the variables). The empirical variance is a measure of the dispersion of the variables around zero. The empirical covariance between the two variables is a measure of how the two variables move together. It is defined as the sum of the products of the samples of two variables divided by the number of samples. In other words, the empirical covariance is the empirical average of the products of the two variables. Empirical correlation is empirical covariance normalized with (i.e., divided by) the square root of the individual empirical variances.

If the two variables have nonzero means, we simply subtract the mean. For example, we define the variance as the expectation of the variable minus the mean and the covariance as the expectation of the product of the differences of each variable minus the respective means. The empirical variances and covariances are formed by subtracting the empirical mean, defined as the sum of the samples divided by the number of samples.

If k variables are given, we can form a $k \times k$ matrix whose entries are the variances and covariances of each pair of the given variables. We can also form a matrix whose entries are the correlations of each pair of variables. The empirical variances, covariances, and correlations as defined here are *estimators* of the true variances, covariances, and correlations.

The empirical variance–covariance and empirical correlation matrices are noisy, but a number of techniques can be used to make estimates more robust. We describe one such technique, a method based on principal-component analysis (PCA).[80]

To understand PCA, a concrete example will be useful. In this example, the series are formed by the returns of k stocks on n trading days. The empirical variance–covariance matrix of these returns is computed as described earlier in this section. We

---

[79]In the last decade, however, scientists working on stochastic resonance have discovered that sometimes *adding* noise might actually allow the extraction of more information. To our knowledge, the implications of stochastic resonance for financial econometrics have not yet been clarified.

[80]For a detailed treatment of PCA and its applications, see Focardi and Fabozzi (2004).

can construct arbitrary portfolios of k stocks, in which the portfolio weights of individual securities sum to 1. Each arbitrary portfolio has a determined variance, and different portfolios have different variances. Although not immediately obvious, it can be demonstrated mathematically that there is a portfolio with maximum variance.

Next, consider all portfolios that are uncorrelated with the maximum-variance portfolio (actually the number is infinite even if the stocks are all positively correlated). We can repeat the previous reasoning and find the maximum-variance portfolio among these portfolios. Repeating this process k times, we can determine k mutually uncorrelated portfolios with decreasing variances.

To illustrate this process, we performed a PCA of the daily returns of 495 stocks in the MSCI Europe Index in the four-year period from January 2000 through December 2003. **Figure 9.3** shows the decay of the variances in the mutually uncorrelated portfolios.[81] The variance decays rapidly, and only the first 15–20 portfolios have a significant variance; the variances of all other portfolios are close to zero.

Figure 9.3. Decay of Variance of Mutually Uncorrelated Portfolios: PCA of Daily Returns of 495 Stocks in the MSCI Europe Index, January 2000– December 2003

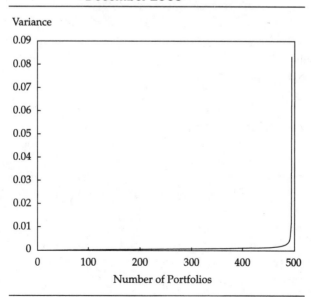

---

[81] A set of mutually uncorrelated portfolios is called a set of "orthogonal portfolios."

The returns of these portfolios form k new time series. The variance–covariance matrix of these series is a diagonal matrix—that is, only the elements on the diagonal are nonzero. A key result in linear algebra is that the original time series can be recovered as linear combinations of the new series. In other words, we started with k series of returns, we formed k mutually uncorrelated portfolios, and we concluded that all original returns are linear combinations of the returns of these portfolios.

A particularly interesting aspect of this construction is that an approximate representation of the original returns can be recovered by considering only those portfolios that have a large variance. Figure 9.3 shows that only 15–20 uncorrelated portfolios have a nonnegligible variance. We can select these portfolios and express each original series as a linear regression on the time series of the returns of these portfolios. This construction is interesting and useful: All the covariances and correlations are now determined solely by their dependence on common portfolios—also referred to as "common factors." In fact, we can now express all our original time series as regressions on a restricted set of common factors. The resulting covariance and correlation matrices determined by PCA contain less noise and are, therefore, more appropriate for portfolio allocation purposes.

Estimation of Regression Models

As discussed in Chapter 8, linear regression is the workhorse of equity modeling. Estimation of regression models is typically performed by using OLS methods. OLS produces estimators that are algebraic expressions of the data. In the two-dimensional xy plane, the OLS method can easily be understood: For a set of xy pairs, one can calculate the straight line in the xy plane that minimizes the sum of the squares of the distance from the line to each pair. To illustrate the OLS method, we randomly generated 500 points and, using the OLS method, fitted the best straight line. **Figure 9.4** shows the cloud of points and the best straight line.

It has been proven that the estimators of the regression parameters determined in this way are optimal linear estimators. Under the assumption that the residuals are normally distributed, the OLS estimators of regression parameters coincide with the ML estimators. The ML estimators are obtained by first computing the residuals with respect to a generic regression and then evaluating the likelihood. The likelihood is obtained by computing the value of a normal distribution on the residuals. The likelihood is then minimized.

Now, suppose we want to estimate the linear regression of one dependent time series on one or more independent time series. At each time step, we observe a sample of the linear regression to be estimated. However, there may be one complication: Residuals might be autocorrelated. The autocorrelation of residuals does not invalidate the standard OLS estimators, but it makes them less efficient and thus not optimal for small samples. Corrections that take into account the autocorrelation have been suggested and can be easily applied—provided one knows how to determine the autocorrelations of residuals.

Figure 9.4. Cloud of 500 Points and the Best-Fitting Straight Line Determined by Using the OLS Method

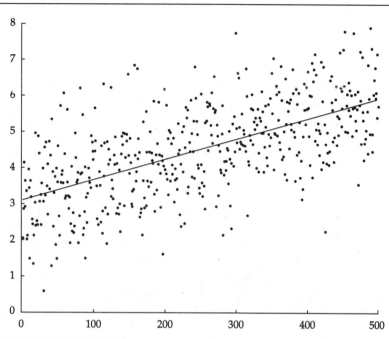

The asymptotic sampling distribution of regression parameters (i.e., the distribution of regression parameters estimated on large samples) can be easily determined. In large samples, regression parameters are normally distributed, with mean and variance that are simple algebraic functions of data.

The estimates of a regression can be made robust. Robustness can be achieved by replacing the standard OLS estimators with estimators that are less sensitive to outliers (that is, to sample values much larger than the bulk of sample data).

Although linear regressions are simple statistical constructs, the analysis and eventual improvement of their performance is delicate. The achievement of robustness and performance of a linear regression hinges on our ability to (1) identify a set of optimal regressors and (2) partition the samples to improve performance.

Consider first the identification of a set of optimal regressors. Simply increasing the number of regressors is not a good strategy because by adding regressors, we increase the number of parameters that must be estimated. Adding regressors also augments the noise of all estimated parameters. Therefore, each additional regressor must be understood and its contribution must be evaluated.

We can determine the importance of a regressor by calculating the ratio of the variance explained by that regressor to total variance. A regressor that explains only a small fraction of the variance has little explanatory power and can be omitted. To gauge the total effect of adding or removing a regressor, one can use a *penalty function* that grows with the number of regressors. In this function, the eventual contribution of an additional regressor is penalized to take into account the overall negative effect of estimating more parameters. This type of analysis is performed by most statistical software packages.

Clustering the sample data achieves different objectives. For example, the clustering of sample data corresponds to the need to make estimates more robust by averaging regression parameters estimated on different clusters. This approach is the basic idea behind the techniques of *shrinkage* and *random coefficient models*.[82] Alternatively, to improve performance, regressions might be made *contextual*. That is, for example, a given predictor of returns might be particularly effective in a specific context, such as a particular market segment or in particular market conditions (Sorensen, Hua, and Qian 2005).

Clearly, despite the intrinsic simplicity of the model, designing and estimating linear regressions is a delicate statistical (and, ultimately, economic) problem. It entails one of the critical issues in testing and modeling—the ever-present trade-offs among model complexity, model risk, and model performance. These trade-offs are a major theme throughout this monograph. Increasing the dimensionality of the model (for example, by adding regressors) makes it more powerful but also makes the model noisier and thus "riskier."

Estimation of Vector Autoregressive Models

In principle, VAR models are kinds of regression models, so estimating VAR models is similar to regression estimation. Some VAR models are subject to restrictions, however, that require the use of special techniques. The simplest case is estimating unrestricted stable VAR models. An unrestricted model is a model in which the parameters are allowed to take any value that results from the estimation process. A model is restricted if its parameters can assume values only in specified ranges.

As explained in Chapter 8, a VAR model is considered to be stable if its solutions are stationary—that is, if the mean, variance, and covariances of its solutions do not change over time. Stability conditions of a VAR model are expressed through conditions that must be satisfied by its parameters—that is, coefficients of every stable model satisfy certain conditions. In particular, stability conditions require solutions to be exponentials with exponent less than 1 in modulus.

Stable VAR models can be estimated by using standard LS and ML methods. In fact, a VAR model is a linear regression of its variables over their own lagged values plus error terms. Clearly, all such variables can be grouped together and residuals can be expressed in terms of data and model parameters. If the residuals are uncorrelated, we can then use multivariate LS methods to minimize the sum of

---

[82]See Chapters 8 and 17 in Fabozzi, Focardi, and Kolm (2006a).

squared residuals as a function of the model parameters. As a result, if we arrange the sample data in appropriate vectors and matrices, we can express the estimators of the model parameters as algebraic functions that involve solely matrix operations, such as inversion and multiplication. These estimators are implemented in commercial software programs.[83]

If we make specific assumptions about the distribution of residuals, we can also use ML methods. In particular, if the model residuals are normally distributed, the ML model estimators coincide with the LS estimators.

If the VAR model is not stable, unrestricted LS methods might still be usable. In dealing with an unstable VAR model, however, one is generally interested in testing and estimating cointegrating relationships, as discussed in Chapter 8. Recall that a cointegrating relationship is a stationary linear combination of the process variables. Taking into account cointegrating relationships in estimating a VAR model cannot be done with standard ML regression methods. The cointegrating relationships impose complicated restrictions on the likelihood function that must be maximized. State-of-the-art ML-based estimation methods for cointegrated systems use a complicated procedure to eliminate constraints from the likelihood function (see Johansen 1991; Banerjee and Hendry 1992). Other methodologies have been proposed, including one based on PCA that is applicable to large data sets.

Bayesian VARs (BVARs) are VAR models estimated by Bayesian methods. When applied to VAR models, Bayesian estimates start from *a priori* distribution of the model parameters. In practice, this distribution embodies a formulation of an idealized model. The *a priori* distribution is then multiplied by the likelihood function, computed as usual by using ML methods. The resulting so-called *a posteriori* likelihood is maximized.

Perhaps the best known BVAR is the model proposed by Litterman (1986). The essence of the Litterman model is that any financial VAR model is a perturbation of a multivariate random walk. The Litterman model determines the *a priori* distribution so that the average of this distribution is simply a random walk. The likelihood function updates the *a priori* distribution, and the result is maximized. Because it requires that the solutions of estimated VAR models do not deviate much from a random walk, the Litterman model is robust.

Extending Bayesian estimates to cointegrated VAR models is not straightforward. The problem is that one has to impose a cointegration structure as an *a priori* distribution. A number of solutions to this problem have been proposed, but none of them has obtained the general acceptance enjoyed by BVARs.

---

[83] Such as those from MATLAB, SAS, and SPSS.

Estimation of Linear Hidden-Variable Models

As discussed in Chapter 8, hidden-variable models include linear state-space models in various formulations and nonlinear models—in particular, Markov switching–VAR (MS–VAR) models.

Linear State-Space Models. Because they include variables that are not observed but must be estimated, state-space models cannot be estimated by using standard regression techniques. A crucial component in estimating state-space models is a tool to filter data known as the "Kalman filter."[84] It is a recursive computational algorithm that, assuming that the model is known, estimates the states from the data. It was conceived in the 1960s to solve the problem of estimating true data—in particular, the position of an aircraft or a missile—from noisy measurements.

Estimating state-space models is done through two general methodologies: ML-based methods and subspace methods. ML-based methods compute the likelihood function of the state-space model that includes hidden variables. Hidden variables are then estimated from the data by using the Kalman filter and the assumption of an unknown generic model. The result is a likelihood function that is expressed as a function of only the unknown model parameters. Maximizing this likelihood yields the estimators.

Subspace methods are technical. They estimate the states by using the Kalman filter, divide the sample data into two sections (conventionally called the "past" and the "future"), and then perform a regression of the future on the past.[85]

Dynamic factor models are a version of state-space models. Several other estimation methods have been proposed, including estimating the equivalent state-space model and the use of PCA-based methods.

Robust Estimation Methods for Linear Models. These estimation methods for VAR models are not intrinsically robust and do not scale well to large systems that are common in finance. Litterman's BVAR is a robust model but can be applied only to small systems (e.g., systems made up of indices). Making VAR estimates robust in the case of a large system requires reducing the dimensionality of the model, which calls for factor models and, in particular, dynamic factor models of prices or returns.

Estimation of Nonlinear Hidden-Variable Models

In discussing the estimation of nonlinear hidden-variable models, we focus on the MS–VAR models because the generalized autoregressive conditional

[84]See Kalman (1960). The Kalman filter is sometimes called the "Kalman–Bucy filter" because of the extension by Kalman and Bucy (1961).
[85]For more on the justification and the advantages of subspace methods, see Chapter 16 in Fabozzi, Focardi, and Kolm (2006a).

heteroscedasticity (GARCH) family of nonlinear hidden-variable models is rarely used in equity modeling. MS–VAR models, however, are being adopted to model regime changes.

Because nonlinear MS–VAR models have hidden variables, their estimation presents the same difficulties as does the estimation of linear state-space models. And for nonlinear MS–VAR models, no equivalent of the Kalman filter exists. Estimation techniques for MS–VAR models typically use the expectation-maximization algorithm (often referred to as the "EM" algorithm) used by Hamilton (1996) in his regime-shift model.[86]

Conclusion

Estimation is the process that determines the parameters of a model. Many estimation methods are available—least-squares, maximum-likelihood, and Bayesian methods. Estimators, being functions of sample data, are random variables. If many parameters need to be estimated, the results will be noisy. Robust estimation methods produce estimates with the minimum possible level of noise. These methods are very important today for many financial applications, such as producing the inputs to sophisticated portfolio optimization systems that are sensitive to noise.

---

[86] See also Chapter 16 in Fabozzi, Focardi, and Kolm (2006a).

10. Practical Considerations When Using Optimization Software

The concept of optimization is fundamental to finance theory. The mean–variance framework, first presented by Markowitz and discussed in Chapter 2, demonstrates that the theory of portfolio selection is about achieving an optimal trade-off between risk and return. In practice, portfolio allocation models often involve more complicated functional forms and constraints than the classical mean–variance optimization problem. The inclusion of transaction costs and taxes adds yet another level of complexity.

Today, numerical software for solving many different types of problems encountered by portfolio managers is widely available both publicly and commercially. This software makes modeling and problem solving simpler and more convenient. A portfolio manager can apply financial models by using modeling languages and software packages or by using numerical subroutine libraries. Many software packages geared toward standard asset allocation or security selection do not require any complicated programming at all but, rather, rely on user input through intuitive graphical interfaces.

A manager has to be careful, however, when using numerical routines as "black boxes." Despite available documentation, understanding exactly what methods and techniques sophisticated numerical subroutines may use is often difficult. The incorrect use of numerical software may reduce efficiency, destroy robustness, and result in a loss of accuracy. Or it may simply produce the wrong conclusions. In this chapter, we provide some guidelines for solving optimization problems with software.[87]

Optimization

The area of optimization is highly technical, and we do not aspire to provide a theoretical treatment of it in this monograph. The tools for optimization modeling come from the field of mathematical programming—more broadly, from operations

---

[87]The discussion in this chapter draws from Chapter 6 in Fabozzi, Focardi, and Kolm (2006a), which provides a discussion of the basic workings of various types of optimization algorithms and focuses on an intuitive understanding of the subject. The chapter covers the simplex algorithm, line-search methods, Newton-type methods, barrier and interior point methods, sequential quadratic programming, and combinatorial and integer programming. In addition, the authors survey the most commonly used publicly and commercially available optimization software.

research. These fields are devoted to the study of the theoretical properties of and practical solution techniques for optimization problems of various forms.

An *optimization problem* consists of three basic components:

- an objective function,
- a set of unknown variables, and
- a set of constraints.

The objective function is a mathematical expression of what the modeler wants to optimize (minimize or maximize) and depends on the unknown decision variables. For example, in the classical mean–variance framework, the *objective function* is to maximize a portfolio's expected return less risk aversion multiplied by portfolio risk. In this case, the *unknown variables* are the portfolio weights, and they may be *constrained* (for example, to be positive and sum to 1).

Constraints may be provided for all or a subset of the unknown decision variables. Constraints are of two kinds: equality constraints and inequality constraints. Equality constraints are constraints that have to hold *with equality* (for example, "the sum of the portfolio weights must equal 1"). Inequality constraints are restrictions of the form "less than or equal to" or "greater than or equal to." For example, a portfolio manager might want to limit exposure of the portfolio to the telecommunications industry to no more than 6 percent of the total portfolio value or might want to make sure that the portfolio invests at least 20 percent in bonds.

In practice, portfolio managers encounter situations in which optimizing several objectives simultaneously might be desirable. For example, in Chapter 2, we mentioned portfolio optimization with higher moments; that is, a portfolio manager might want to maximize the mean and the skewness while minimizing the variance and the kurtosis. Optimization problems with multiple objectives are typically reformulated as a problem with a single objective and then transformed into a standard optimization problem.

In general, the solutions to an optimization problem are of two types: *global* and *local*. The global maximum (minimum) solution is the global maximum (or minimum) of the objective function over the whole range on which the function is defined. A local maximum (minimum) solution is a point at which the objective function is larger (smaller) than all other points in its vicinity. In most cases, it is the global solution that the manager is ultimately solving for. Complicated objective functions, however, may have multiple local optimal solutions. The difficulty in these cases is that the manager must find all the local solutions to determine which one is the global solution.

Most efficient modern optimization algorithms available today attempt to find only a local solution because finding a global optimal solution is difficult. To locate all local optimal solutions and then choose the best one requires an exhaustive search. No general efficient algorithm for the global optimization problem is currently available; the specialized algorithms rely on unique properties of the objective function and constraints. Fortunately, most optimization problems encountered in portfolio management have one unique optimal solution; in such a case, the local solution is the same as the global solution.

Optimization problems are classified according to the functional form of the objective function and the constraints. Researchers have identified a basic set of optimization problems, which are considered the *standard* forms. Some of the most common standard forms are linear programs, quadratic programs, convex programs, conic programs, and nonlinear programs. For portfolio allocation applications, the optimization problems often take the form of quadratic or convex programs. For instance, classic Markowitz mean–variance optimization is a quadratic program.

An important property of quadratic, convex, and conic programs is that they have a unique solution. That is, in this case, the local optimal solutions are indeed also global optimal solutions.

Today, optimization packages are built on sophisticated algorithms. Thus, learning and understanding in detail how particular algorithms work is hard for the nonexpert. And although a basic understanding of how they work is useful, such knowledge is often unnecessary if one's goal is simply to make efficient use of optimization software. The next section introduces how one can work with optimization software to efficiently solve a particular problem.

Solving Optimization Problems

The solution process for an optimization problem can be divided into three parts: (1) formulating the problem, (2) choosing an optimizer, and (3) solving the problem with the optimizer.

Formulating the Problem. Numerical optimization software has been developed for various standard forms. Therefore, in solving an optimization problem with numerical software, the first step is to identify the problem's form. This step is straightforward if the problem has already been given in one of the standard forms. Generally, however, the specific problem has to be transformed into the appropriate form. As long as a particular optimization problem can be reformulated into one of the standard forms, the portfolio manager is set.

Choosing an Optimizer. Choosing and purchasing optimization software can be costly and time-consuming because evaluating the various solvers for the specific applications in mind requires careful, systematic testing. Some solvers work better for a certain type of problem than others do. Unfortunately, no single technique is better or outperforms all the others for all problems. Often, the only way to find out how well a solver works for a particular problem is through extensive testing. Expecting to find a single software package that will solve all one's optimization problems is also unrealistic. Different approaches and software packages may, however, be complementary. In practice, the recommendation is to try various algorithms on the same problem to see which one performs best as far as speed, accuracy, and stability are concerned.

Most optimization software is designed to handle prototypical mathematical programs or types in some standard form. The optimization algorithms or software for the various standard forms create a toolbox that can be used to solve a particular part of a problem. Not every problem can be solved with a hammer alone; some may also require a drill and a screwdriver. Although a simple linear program can be solved with a general nonlinear programming algorithm, doing so is not a good idea. The portfolio manager should always try to use software targeted to the specific problem. By doing so, the manager will be able to solve the problem not only faster but also more accurately.

   ▪ *Constraints.* Whether a problem is constrained or unconstrained will affect the choice of algorithm or technique used for its solution. In general, unconstrained optimization is somewhat simpler than constrained optimization, but the types of constraints also matter. Problems with equality constraints are generally easier to deal with than those with inequality constraints, as are linear constraints compared with nonlinear constraints.

   ▪ *Derivatives.* Many optimization routines use derivative information.[88] Therefore, the software needs to be able to access or compute the derivatives of the objective function and the constraints. Thus, some or all of the first-order derivatives (and sometimes also second-order derivatives) of the objective function and constraints should be available as analytic expressions. If they are not, the algorithm will have to calculate these derivatives numerically, which is more time-consuming. Supplying the analytic derivatives will greatly speed up the solution process. In most instances, supplying the analytic derivatives will also increase the numerical stability and accuracy of the algorithm.

   ▪ *Dense vs. sparse and medium vs. large problems.* When many decision variables are involved (for nonlinear problems, "many" means more than a few thousand, and for linear problems, "many" means more than a hundred thousand), the problem is referred to as a "large-scale" optimization problem. For efficiency reasons, large-scale numerical algorithms try to take advantage of the specific structure in a problem. For example, so-called *sparse matrix techniques* are used instead of *dense matrix calculations*, if possible, to improve the efficiency of the linear algebra computations inside the routines.

   ▪ *User interface and settings.* If a mathematical programming modeling language is used, an optimization problem can be specified on a much higher level (much closer to the original mathematical formulation) than if a lower-level

---

[88]Here, we refer to the mathematical meaning of "derivative" (i.e., the instantaneous rate of change of a function), which is unrelated to the financial meaning of the word.

programming language (much further away from the original mathematical formulation) is used.[89] Furthermore, by making the user interface and the mathematical programming formulation independent of a particular optimizer, a portfolio manager obtains flexibility and portability for the model. Portability will facilitate testing the model with different optimizers.

Good optimization software allows a portfolio manager to specify various options and settings of the algorithms, such as the maximum number of iterations or function evaluations allowed and the convergence criteria and tolerances.

Many optimization platforms also provide a preoptimization phase. During this phase, the manager analyzes the problem to select the best and most suitable algorithm. Normally, software support is also available for checking the correctness of the analytically supplied derivatives by comparing them with numerical approximations.

Solving the Problem with the Optimizer. The final step of solving the problem with the optimizer requires establishing a starting vector, running the software, and analyzing the results.

■ *Choose the starting vector.* Some optimizers expect a starting vector. It should be the portfolio manager's best guess of the optimal solution. For some problems, a natural candidate for a good starting point is easy to find. For example, the analytical solution of a simplified problem sometimes works well. In general, however, choosing the starting point is difficult. In using optimizers that provide support in generating a good starting point, the manager would be wise to let the algorithm choose, unless the portfolio manager knows that her or his information is superior. Numerical testing should confirm this.

■ *Run the software and monitor progress.* Optimization algorithms are of an iterative nature. That is, the algorithm, or the "solver," generates a sequence of approximate solutions that gets closer and closer to the true solution at each step. Because the true solution is not known, however, and the solver cannot go on indefinitely, the portfolio manager stops the iterative process when a termination criterion is satisfied. One of the more common convergence criteria is when the difference between two approximate solutions is smaller than a tolerance that the manager has prespecified.

A portfolio manager can obtain valuable information by monitoring the progress of the optimization process. In particular, the number of iterations and function evaluations tells a manager how quickly the problem is converging. To some extent, the sizes of constraint and first-order optimality condition violations (standard outputs of an optimization algorithm as it is running) convey how far away the process is from reaching the optimal point. The sizes of the *Lagrange*

---

[89]Some examples of higher-level model languages are AMPL, GAMS, MATLAB, Mathematica, and LINGO. C, C++, C#, and Fortran are examples of low-level languages.

multipliers provide information on which constraints are most binding and on the sensitivity of the value of the objective function to the various constraints.[90]

■ *Analyze the results.* Even if the optimizer converges and produces a solution, the analyst should not blindly believe that the output is correct. The best way to understand how a particular software behaves is through experimentation. Indeed, understanding the behavior of software is necessary for making practical decisions about algorithm selection and to confirm that the results are valid. A good approach is to rerun the optimization with more stringent settings (e.g., smaller convergence tolerances) and evaluate whether the problem still converges. If several optimizers are available, the analyst can compare the results generated by each one.

To make sure that the software is working correctly, good practice is to begin by solving a simple problem that has a known solution. Sometimes, an analyst does not know whether the problem at hand has a single local optimal solution or multiple local optimal solutions. A simple way to check is to rerun the optimizer with different starting values. If they all converge to the same solution, then the analyst has probably found the unique solution.

By having a computer model of the problem, an analyst can test how sensitive the outputs are to changes in the inputs. In the case of mean–variance optimization, an analyst can study how the solution (the optimal solution) changes as slight changes are made in expected return and covariance forecasts. A simple experiment of this kind will show how sensitive the portfolio allocation model is to measurement errors in the forecasts. If the results are sensitive to small changes, this may indicate that the model is misspecified or ill posed. However, many financial optimization models are sensitive to small changes in inputs, and in these cases, robust formulations often offer a good alternative.

Optimization Software

Commercially and publicly provided optimization software is available. Optimization software packages that have been developed specifically for portfolio management applications are provided by Axioma, Barra, ITG, and Northfield Information Services.[91] Readers who are seeking an optimizer to perform mean–variance optimization on a set of securities will typically find this category of optimizers, which does not require the use of any programming language, to fully satisfy their needs.

---

[90]The classical approach to solving constrained optimization problems is the method of Lagrange multipliers. This approach converts the constrained optimization problem into an unconstrained one by introducing artificial variables referred to as Lagrange multipliers.

[91]See, respectively, www.axiomainc.com, www.barra.com, www.itginc.com, and www. northinfo.com.

Asset-class optimizers are a class of commercially available portfolio optimizers that are "stripped down"—that is, they do not have the flexibility or power to handle large numbers of securities but they can optimize across a limited number of asset classes. These optimizers are typically less expensive (and also easier to use) than security-level optimizers. Asset-class optimizers are provided by, for example, APT, Efficient Solutions, Ibbotson Associates, Insightful Corporation, with the AIG SunAmerica (Polaris), Wagner Math Finance, and Sungard (WealthStation). New Frontier Advisors' ROM Optimizer uses resampling to reduce the impact of estimation error on outputs, and one version of the Ibbotson optimizer uses a different resampling technique to accomplish a similar objective. The Ibbotson optimizer also has a Bayesian (specifically, Black–Litterman) function. WealthStation, which is Web-based software for financial advisors serving high-net-worth clients, offers tools for viewing and managing investors' diverse assets and for generating client-specific reports.

Much of the material we've covered in this chapter applies to more advanced problem solving. Although noncommercial optimization packages are typically slower than the best commercial optimization packages, they often provide more flexibility and extendibility for advanced problem solving because the source code can often be obtained. This feature is especially important for users who want to develop customized solvers. In some noncommercial libraries, however, the documentation is sparse at best. If thorough documentation is important, the portfolio manager should check for it.

Because optimization software is sophisticated, it can be difficult for the nonexpert to use. Today, however, most optimization packages can be accessed in user-friendly modeling language that provides a convenient interface for specifying problems and that automates many of the underlying mathematical and algorithmic details. In particular, a modeling language allows the user to specify particular optimization problems in a generic fashion that is independent of the specific algorithmic and to input requirements of optimization routines. Popular modeling languages are AMPL and GAMS. [92] Online *optimization software guides* are good starting points for selecting suitable optimization software. [93]

The NEOS Server for Optimization provides free Internet access to more than 50 optimization software packages that can solve a large class of unconstrained and nonlinearly constrained optimization problems. [94] Optimization problems can be submitted online in a programming language, modeling language, or a wide variety of other low-level data formats. The NEOS Server provides a great testing platform.

---

[92] AMPL is described at www.ampl.com, and GAMS, at www.gams.com.

[93] See, for example, the "NEOS Guide" (www-fp.mcs.anl.gov/otc/Guide/index.html), the "Decision Tree for Optimization Software" (plato.asu.edu/guide.html), and Chapter 6 in Fabozzi, Focardi, and Kolm (2006a).

[94] See www-neos.mcs.anl.gov and Czyzyk, Mesnier, and Moré (1998).

Standard spreadsheet programs, such as Microsoft Excel and Corel Quattro Pro, are equipped with general-purpose optimization algorithms for linear, integer, and nonlinear programming problems. These routines work well for small-scale problems (up to a few hundred decision variables) but are less suited for larger problems.

GNU Octave and MATLAB are two high-level technical computing and interactive environments for model development, data visualization, data analysis, and numerical simulation.[95] ILOG CPLEX, LINDO, MOSEK, and XPRESS-MP are robust and efficient commercial optimizers for large linear and convex quadratic programming.[96]

---

[95] Available at, respectively, www.octave.org and www.mathworks.com.

[96] Available at, respectively, www.ilog.com/products/cplex, www.lindo.com, www.mosek.com, and www.dashopt.com.

11. Models in Practice: Industry Survey Results

To understand how the industry evaluates some of the techniques discussed in this monograph and to what degree these techniques are actually being used in equity portfolio management, The Intertek Group spent the summer of 2005 interviewing 21 people responsible for quantitative methods at firms in North America and Europe.[97] Participants represented firms responsible for a total of US$4 trillion in assets under management, of which roughly 50 percent was invested in equities at that time. Two-thirds of the firms are among the largest money managers in their respective markets, and one-third represent medium-size firms and/or quantitatively oriented organizations. Six are U.S. firms and fifteen are European firms. The geographical distribution of the European firms is as follows: France, two; Germany, three; Italy, two; the Netherlands, one; Sweden, one; Switzerland, four; and the United Kingdom, two.

The survey covered three areas in equity portfolio management: (1) return forecasting, (2) model-risk (that is, the risk of error in model selection) mitigation, and (3) optimization. In each area, participants were asked what evaluation (if any) they had made of a given technique and whether it was being used in practice.[98]

The survey built on the 2000/2001 and 2003 Intertek studies of quantitative methods in asset management, for which The Intertek Group interviewed more than 150 people in North America and Europe.[99] A comparison of the results of the 2005 survey with the previous Intertek survey results indicates that forecasting techniques are playing a bigger role in the asset management process today than in the recent past. In the 2000/2001 survey, most sources found that the major advantage of modeling was "to bring discipline to the investment process." Quantitative methods were used primarily to measure risk, with models assessing exposure to a number of factors. Only a small number of firms were using models to predict returns.

The active asset managers interviewed for the earlier surveys apparently believed that they could use judgment and intuition to predict the market, although the mainstream academic opinion at the time was that models can assess risk but

---

[97]The survey reported in this chapter was conducted by Caroline Jonas of The Intertek Group.
[98]The survey results for the use of modeling in the management of defined-benefit pension funds in the United States and Europe is described in Fabozzi, Focardi, and Jonas (2005).
[99]Results of the earlier surveys for European firms are described in Fabozzi, Focardi, and Jonas (2004).

©2006, The Research Foundation of CFA Institute

cannot predict expected returns.[100] Recent research, however, has shown that markets are to some extent predictable. Many firms are now trying to exploit this predictability by using models to forecast expected returns. Of the 21 firms surveyed in 2005, 18 use models to predict returns. A trend found in the 2003 study toward the use of multiple models was confirmed by this latest survey. Together with a renewed interest in forecasting has come increased attention to robust optimization (optimization that is relatively insensitive to errors in inputs) and model-risk mitigation. Both are a confirmation that forecasting models are now used in practice. In the previous surveys, we found that optimization techniques were not widely used: They were considered to be too brittle (that is, too sensitive to changes in the inputs) and prone to "error maximization." This survey, however, found a strong interest in methods for improving the reliability of optimizers. Similar considerations apply to model-risk mitigation: Once considered an area of academic research, model risk mitigation techniques are now being used at a number of the more quantitatively oriented organizations.

The next three sections present details of our findings in the areas of return forecasting, model-risk mitigation, and optimization. A summary of the number of firms responding that they used a given technique is provided in **Table 11.1.**

Equity Return-Forecasting Techniques

Among the firms surveyed, simple methods with a clear link to economic intuition are typically preferred. Momentum and reversal models are the most widely used techniques, but many sources remarked that the bread and butter of their modeling effort was regression on predictors of stock returns, such as financial ratios. A frequent comment was the desire of analysts to combine company fundamentals (regression on predictors) with market sentiment (momentum/reversal models). Autoregressive, cointegration, state-space, regime-switching, and nonlinear methods (such as neural networks and decision trees) play an important, sometimes central, role at some firms. The survey also revealed a growing interest in the use of high-frequency (more frequent than daily) data in asset management.

Models Based on Exogenous Predictors.
Models based on exogenous predictors (e.g., models that regress future returns on current company financial ratios) are widely used. For a number of firms, this modeling technique is the core of their return-forecasting effort. A U.S. source that uses ratios derived from financial statements to predict future stock returns commented, "We use these ratios extensively in our bottom-up equity model and categorize them into different categories, such as operating efficiency, financial strength, earnings quality, capital expenditures."

---

[100]Perhaps this difference in attitudes can be explained by the fact that most modeling efforts in the 1990s were related to valuation of derivatives.

Table 11.1. Summary of Survey Results
(21 firms)

Technique	Number of Firms	Percentage of Firms
Equity return forecasting		
Models based on exogenous predictors	13	62%
Momentum models	17	81
Reversal models	18	86
Cointegration models	7	33
Markov-switching/regime-switching models	2	10
Autoregressive models	5	24
State-space models	1	5
Nonlinear models	4	19
Models of higher-moment dynamics	2	10
Model-risk mitigation		
Bayesian estimation	2	10
Averaging/shrinkage	5	24
Random coefficient models	1	5
Optimization		
Robust optimization	7	33
Multistage stochastic optimization	2	10

To capture market sentiment, models that capture fundamentals are typically combined with momentum and/or reversal models. A source in Europe remarked, "We use models based on exogenous predictors for valuation, and combine these models with momentum and reversal models. Valuation is necessary, but psychology also plays a role in the market. Look at the long bubble market: If you had based your modeling on valuation only, you would have got killed. You need to add market sentiment to valuation."

Momentum and Reversal Models. Momentum models are intended to capture the persistence of local trends, such as price rises. Reversal models model the inversion of local trends, such as price reversals. Together, momentum and reversal models are the most widely used modeling techniques at the firms surveyed.

Sources frequently noted the problem of high turnover induced by these models and described various techniques, including weighting and penalty functions, designed to mitigate it. Many sources that use both techniques said that they use reversal models less extensively than momentum models. The problem with high turnover is more acute in reversal models than in momentum models. In addition, the precise timing of reversals is a difficulty. One source remarked, "Due to the excessive required turnover of strategies based on short-term price momentum and reversals, we have limited the application in our model."

In contrast to those who advocated the use of momentum/reversal models, a source who had been using various momentum models for some time remarked, "Momentum models have received extensive academic attention in the last 30 years. However, in our experience, the momentum effect has largely become a small-cap-only phenomenon in the last 10 years."

Momentum and reversal are coupled phenomena: If momentum exists, so does reversal. As demonstrated by a number of academic studies, however, complex time dynamics may exist in momentum and reversals that give rise to different patterns of momentum and reversal at different time horizons. Some firms are using multiple time horizons in their momentum/reversal models.

Cointegration Models. Cointegration models, models of short-term dynamics and long-run equilibrium, are being used at one-third of the firms surveyed. Several sources mentioned that cointegration is their core forecasting technique. A source at one firm whose modeling approach is based on cointegration said, "We chose a cointegration approach because the models are based on economic and finance theory and calculated from economic data; they allow a transparent process."

Another source at a European firm where cointegration is being used commented, "The nice thing about cointegration is that you have a good story to tell that makes sense to management—for example, long-term fair value and short-term direction. But there are some problems. Cointegration is not very flexible, and you need very long time series to put a number of variables into models, but if there are too many variables, you have problems with estimation."

In addition, several sources who use cointegration remarked that performance of the models is sensitive to liquidity and volatility.

Markov-Switching/Regime-Switching Models. Markov-switching or regime-switching models have not been widely evaluated by the industry. Detecting the precise timing of a switch is one of the problems with using these techniques. At most firms, judgment is used to assess regime change. One source commented, "Market regime is, of course, taken into consideration in the overall assessment of equity and sector attractiveness, but this is not done in a strictly quantitative way using regime-switching models."

Autoregressive Models. Autoregressive models (models incorporating lagged values) are used in practice at one-fourth of the firms, but the technique has not been widely evaluated. The perception is that autoregression techniques require a lot of resources in terms of data and modeling.

A source at a firm that is using autoregressive models commented, "Autoregressive models are an extension of and a step ahead of momentum models. We are using these quite a bit, though we are not doing fully structured vector autoregressions. Doing so would take a very long time."

Another source remarked, "We are using autoregressive models, but with caution due to the problem of overfitting the market." (Recall from Chapter 7 that overfitting is the fitting of unpredictable noise in small samples.)

State-Space Models. State-space models are not widely known in the industry. These models are used to model hidden variables. Among those surveyed, only one source mentioned using state-space models extensively (for data transformation before analysis). A second source mentioned that the firm is examining these models with a high level of interest.

One source mentioned that, although state-space models were not being used, the firm had considered the models because "state-space models perform interesting tasks in estimating unobserved components of interest"—that is, components that represent interesting market situations.

Nonlinear Methods. Nonlinear methods—such as neural networks, decision trees, and CART (see Chapter 6)—are being used by only one-fifth of the firms surveyed, but half of the firms consider nonlinear methods to have potential in equity return modeling. Obstacles to greater use of nonlinear methods include the lack of theory (although most sources believed that nonlinear methods *do* have explanatory power out of sample), a tendency of these methods toward overfitting, and the firm's lack of the requisite skills in-house.

A source at a European firm that is using nonlinear methods said, "In modeling, one already makes a lot of assumptions that are far from the real world. It makes sense to use nonlinear methods: They are great for nonlinear phenomena where one wants to model extremes together. We use decision trees extensively. They are flexible and dynamic, though they require a lot of parameterization and are quite sensitive to the parameterization. Our experience with decision trees in stock picking has been quite positive, and we are now trying to apply them to other areas."

Models of Higher-Moment Dynamics. Models of the dynamics of higher moments (i.e., variance, skewness, and kurtosis), such as the many variants of generalized autoregressive conditional heteroscedasticity (GARCH) that link volatility and expected returns, are used at fewer than 10 percent of the sources, but interest in optimization with higher moments is growing.

A source at one firm that is using models of higher-moment dynamics said, "GARCH techniques are used in trading, but we also see potential for GARCH in conditional return forecasting."

Another source, one at a firm that is not yet using higher-moment dynamics, remarked, "While volatility is an important factor in our equity multifactor models, we are not yet considering higher moments, even though we are aware of the leptokurtic behavior of many daily return series." (A return distribution is leptokurtic—that is, has leftward kurtosis—if it has a fatter tail on the left side than a normal distribution has.)

Another source commented, "We are in the early stages of experimentation with higher moments. There might well be areas of applicability in equity portfolio management. There is now a growing awareness of the importance of higher moments."

Model-Risk Mitigation Techniques

The issue of model-risk mitigation is gaining attention, but it has not been widely addressed by the industry. A source in one European firm said, "We are not currently using any model-risk mitigation techniques but we are aware of the problem and would like to address it. We are presently considering how to deal with model risk in the covariance matrix and are looking at possible solutions."

The most widely used techniques for model-risk mitigation are Bayesian shrinkage and model averaging. Most firms use several models, and averaging the prediction of different models is only natural. More sophisticated techniques, such as random coefficient models, are not widely used.

Bayesian Estimation. Although Bayesian techniques are considered to be conceptually interesting, the firms surveyed generally consider Bayesian estimation to be hard to use explicitly (many mention using it *implicitly*) and hard to implement. One source that has looked at Bayesian estimation in model-risk mitigation commented, "Bayesian estimation is intuitively appealing but hard to implement as a standard process."

Shrinkage/Averaging. The preferred techniques to mitigate model risk are shrinkage (a Bayesian process of shrinking the predictions of one model toward the predictions of another model) and, in line with the trend toward using multiple models, averaging the results of several models. Shrinkage/averaging techniques are being used at only one-quarter of the firms surveyed (several others have ongoing research projects on the use of such techniques), but those using these techniques consider them necessary, even essential, in reducing model risk.

A source at a European firm that is using averaging techniques remarked, "It is the most common, most sensible approach to model-risk mitigation." Another source at a firm where Bayesian estimation forms the core of the model-risk mitigation effort said, "We also use averaging/shrinkage. We consider it extremely important, necessary."

Random Coefficient Models. Random coefficient models, described in Chapter 8, are not widely known in the industry; few sources mentioned having evaluated the technique. One source in a firm that uses a form of the technique commented, however, that they randomize data to ensure against overfitting.

Optimization Techniques

Roughly half of the firms participating in the survey continue to eschew optimization. A source at a firm that does no optimization said, "Optimization requires elements that are sufficiently reliable for the alpha." "Optimization goes down because of the lack of data in the time series available in finance. Periods such as the TMT [technology, media, telecommunications] bubble demonstrated that it is not possible to manage the risk if you use optimization techniques."

Another source commented, "The problem with any optimization routine is that it is very difficult to identify the forecasting error. If one knew what the forecasting error were, you would not have it in the first place."

Robust Optimization. As firms begin to use forecasting methods in practice, they need to have some optimization technique in place to exploit the correlations determined through the forecasting process. Although a number of firms surveyed perform quadratic, mean–variance, or Markowitz optimization, they do not consider these approaches to be robust.

The robustness of the optimization process is a major concern. One-third of the sources said they are using some form of robust optimization. Some sources pointed out, however, that there is an integration between robust optimization and robust estimation. Several sources cited the use of resampling methods to make robust estimates of the variance–covariance matrix.

Multistage Stochastic Optimization. Multistage stochastic optimization, described in Chapter 3, is being used at 10 percent of the firms surveyed. One source mentioned that the firm has abandoned the technique and is now using robust optimization. Sensitivity to forecasting errors is the main problem.

A source at a firm that is using the Black–Litterman model (see Black and Litterman 1990) commented, "Multistage optimization is too complex; it does not fit the forecasting models."

In the area of optimization, the survey also revealed a strong interest in optimization with higher moments.

Outstanding Issues

Data remain a big issue in modeling. Most sources interviewed agreed that modelers have *enough* data to support even complex models, although quantity of data is still an issue for European small-cap stocks. The problem is one of data *quality*. A source in a European firm remarked, "Data quality has improved tremendously over the past 10 years, but it is still an issue, at least in Europe. The problem is one of combining data from different sources. For example, when companies merge and different data sources treat the entities differently, the data have to be stitched together . . . . It requires a lot of cleaning the data to make them the same."

12. Quantitative Modeling Today and Tomorrow

Modeling of the type we have been discussing has implications for portfolio managers and for the industry in general. We summarize here the state of modeling and, although predicting future developments is notoriously difficult, give our insights on the future direction of modeling in the industry.

Modeling in Portfolio Management

Given the strong competition to manage assets, performance levels that can be achieved by modeling will become a benchmark against which any portfolio manager will be measured. In the previous chapters, we discussed a number of modeling techniques for equity return forecasting and portfolio optimization. And as described in Chapter 11, a survey by the Intertek Group of asset management firms, including many of the largest firms in the world, showed that most firms surveyed do use some forecasting techniques and the use of optimization is growing. Because these firms are among the biggest players in the market, they set the performance benchmarks that other firms must pursue. They also shape the market itself. As a result of the use of sophisticated statistical techniques, the profit opportunities available from the work of human judgment are being reduced, at least in highly liquid markets where data on public companies are abundant and reliable. As we remarked in Chapter 2, profit opportunities are essentially the result of patterns of delayed response; computerized methods can quickly capture these patterns and exploit any profitability. In so doing, they rapidly arbitrage out simple profit opportunities.

The capabilities of computerized systems do not mean, however, that assets will be managed in the future only by computer programs—although completely automatic funds are now possible. For computer management, a number of issues are still outstanding. First is the challenge presented by the data. The input of data from multiple providers can be automated, but human intervention is needed to handle data issues presented by, for example, mergers and acquisitions, stock splits, and other financial operations that affect the data stream of stock prices. In addition, the present level of standardization among data providers is not sufficient to allow completely automatic operations: A lot of data cleaning is required to ensure that data meet the quality standards required for modeling. The bottom line is that running an automatic fund requires a highly trained human supervisor with experience in data handling and an understanding of the details of corporate events. The supervisor oversees the feeding of data into models and can intervene manually when data present problems.

Second, assuming that the data problems are correctly dealt with, an automatic fund requires a forecasting methodology as well as a portfolio strategy. A portfolio strategy is a mechanism that builds portfolios based on forecasts. In its most complete implementation, a portfolio strategy is an optimizer. Both of these components—forecasting methodologies and optimizers—exist and can be integrated automatically. Technically, one can feed data to a forecasting algorithm, feed the resulting forecasts to an optimizer or to some heuristic method, and build a portfolio. This approach is already in use at some firms.

Before entrusting large sums of money to an automatic fund, however, firm managers must be sure that the process is robust. Robustness can be achieved in various ways. A typical approach is to implement layers of controls: The forecasting and optimization methodologies produce outputs that are filtered through one or more layers of risk management. A layered approach, however, presents significant integration challenges. Forecasting models typically work on different principles from those of risk management models. Integrating models has been identified by many heads of quantitative investment as a key modeling challenge.

A layered approach also typically requires a high-level human supervisor (for example, the risk manager) who can make stop-loss decisions or solve conflicts between various layers of control. When asked how he would describe his job, a pilot of transatlantic flights answered, "Long hours of boredom punctuated by instants of sheer terror." Supervising an automatic fund is similar. It requires the ability to make rare interventions should losses surpass established limits. Many asset management firms have stop-loss procedures that interrupt the operations of a fund to avoid excessive losses (with a safe-start function to resume operations after a fund has been stopped). However, such a structure is only a partial solution. What is required is the ability to intervene without stopping active investing—which calls for robust forecasting and optimization methodologies.

Until recently, most efforts in developing robust methodologies were concentrated on the estimation of the variance–covariance matrix because it is the most critical element in the widely used static models. The performance of optimizers depends on it. For static models, estimates of expected returns are less critical than the variance–covariance matrix. In the new generation of dynamic models and optimizers, however, other elements are critical. The estimation of expected returns that vary in time can become noisy, producing unstable optimization results; higher moments, unless explicitly accounted for, may interfere with both estimates and optimization.

What these models require is a global robust methodology that encompasses both estimation and optimization in an integrated process. As explained in Chapter 7, methods currently being used to make estimations more robust include resampling, averaging techniques, and Bayesian methods. In the area of optimization, constraints are being used to increase the robustness of the process. Of the firms surveyed, 33 percent were already using some form of robust optimization; another 14 percent said they were evaluating such techniques for future deployment.

The bottom line is that the safe operation of automatic funds requires robust methods and a residual level of intelligent supervision. Supervision at this level requires much skill. The model supervisor must combine an intimate knowledge of the models and the markets with the ability to detect any performance degradation that cannot be attributed to acceptable statistical fluctuations. Above all, the supervisor must resist the temptation to intervene, to override the model, too often.

Clearly, on top of these necessities, the design team and the model supervisor must be able to adapt models to changing market conditions—the disappearance of old profit patterns and the appearance of new ones. The need to adapt models to a changing market is undoubtedly a weakness from a scientific point of view, but in practice, it is the reality of financial modeling.

State of Modeling in the Industry

Traditionally, one of two money management functions has been used to justify the management fees charged by the industry. On the one hand, asset managers are credited with facilitating investors' access to the market and optimizing the risk–return profile of investments. On the other hand, the argument is that active asset managers are paid for producing returns in excess of what the investors themselves might be able to obtain.

The claim of superior performance has always been controversial. Clearly, the ability to produce returns in excess of the market is not obvious when the industry is, in practice, the market. Although the performances of individual portfolio managers in any given year will differ significantly, numerous studies have thrown doubt on the *persistence* of superior performance.[101]

During the long bull run that closed the 20th century in which markets consistently delivered outstanding returns, investment performance above that of the benchmark was not much of an issue. Since the disappointing performance of the markets following the year 2000, however, the role, function, and cost structure of the asset management industry is being closely scrutinized. The growing diffusion of modeling gives a scientific twist to this debate. Econometric analysis has shown that the market does reflect some predictability. The existing level of predictability, found even in relatively simple strategies published in academic papers, seems to be sufficient to earn an excess return after taking into consideration transaction costs. If, as seems to be the case, a growing number of asset managers attempt to exploit

---

[101] See Rhodes (2000); Kazemi, Schneeweis, and Pancholi (2003).

this predictability with sophisticated statistical programs, however, the ability to earn excess returns will be reduced, at least until profitable predictability is found in new strategies.

In addition to allowing one to identify profit opportunities in developed markets, quantitative methods can increase efficiency in investment management firms. This boon is certainly the motivation that firms implementing quantitative management cite. Quantitative methods also facilitate the matching of risk and returns to investor preferences. Given the advantages that quantitative methods offer, the march toward modeling seems irreversible, at least in managing investments in liquid markets where quality data are abundant.

How, then, do asset management firms introduce the models that will allow them to identify profit opportunities and increase efficiency? For firms not born as quantitative boutiques, the typical pattern so far is one of progressive introduction. A firm decides to begin to experiment with quantitative techniques and chooses a methodology on the basis of the firm's views and its ability to control the experiment. Usually, after starting with simple functions, additional statistical functionality is added—for example, the evaluation of correlations or the analysis of momentum and reversals.

When the firm has acquired sufficient confidence in a given technique, typically by running a fund offline for a period of months, it entrusts a small amount of money to the fund and takes it live. The performance of the fund is tracked against that of other funds, and if the automated fund is successful, the firm transfers increasing amounts of assets to it. Indeed, some asset management firms surveyed by Intertek went entirely quantitative after comparing performance for several years and finding that the quantitatively managed funds produced the more positive and more stable results. Obviously, not every experience produces the same happy result. Other paths to introducing quantitative methods are possible.

According to the Intertek survey, most asset management firms now have some sort of ranking/screening system that orients and constrains the choices a manager of a quantitative portfolio can make. Using such decision-making systems as ranking and screening is essentially different, however, from using a full-fledged quantitative approach.

In the end, if and how a firm moves toward modeling is a function of its culture and structure, the markets in which it operates, the level of computer and mathematical literacy of its managers, and the skills available in the market.

The integration of a full-fledged quantitative approach with human judgment has been and still is a central theme in financial modeling. Although human agents can perform complex intellectual tasks, they can handle only a limited amount of information—in particular, only a limited amount of statistical information. Models thrive on masses of statistical information. For example, a human agent cannot easily evaluate and effectively use the 45 correlation numbers that describe the correlation structure of 10 sectors, but a computer can easily handle such rich correlation structures. But although computerized models can exploit statistical regularities that cannot be handled by humans, humans bring firsthand experience with markets and securities that can be critical in some market conditions. Several techniques were designed specifically for this purpose—for example, Bayesian methods such as the Black–Litterman framework (see Black and Litterman 1991; Litterman 2003)—and are being used in the industry. Other methodologies have been developed to facilitate the interaction of humans with models, including sophisticated visualization tools that personalize the presentation of data and "query tools" for "drilling down" so that various aggregates of the data can be constructed on demand.

Today's modeling efforts in the industry are typically of an econometric type. They concentrate on predicting returns—analyzing time series, prices, returns, financial ratios, and so on. In a sense, this situation is surprising. One might expect that modeling efforts would be directed at analyzing the external environment to create an accurate picture of the economic relationships between firms, technological innovations, economic development, and so on. One area in which modeling is being used to understand corporate dynamics is credit-risk modeling.

Future Possibilities

An area that is only beginning to be explored by some of the most quantitatively oriented organizations is the automatic handling of unstructured data, such as text, which is currently the domain of judgment (see Leinweber 2003; Focardi and Jonas 2002). Some of the requisite technologies for this endeavor—for example, tagging, keyword searches, and query—are routinely used by data providers to manage information and allow users to manipulate data. But they are only the tip of the iceberg. Standards such as XML (extensible markup language) and RDF (resource description framework) and industry-specific standards now allow the computerized handling of unstructured data. Text mining and related technologies presently allow the analysis of huge amounts of textual information. Although investment management firms are showing little interest in these possibilities, the pressure to realize excess returns and reduce operating costs may lead some firms to seek to integrate the mathematical modeling of time series with the computerized handling of textual information. The standardization promised by the Semantic Web might appear a bit futuristic, but all the technological components are now available.[102] In banking and finance, a reduced "semantic web" might be contained in the ISO 15022 central data repository.

The economic and financial reality behind investment management will dictate future developments in modeling. Ultimately, investor preferences will determine the type of innovations the industry pursues.

---

[102]The Semantic Web, managed by Tim Berners-Lee, is a project to define and link all data on the Web in such a way as to allow automated handling by computers across applications and platforms. It will do so by attaching a descriptive structured metafile to each Web page. For discussion of the Semantic Web, see Fensel, Wahlster, Lieberman, and Hendler (2004) and Daconta, Obrst, and Smith (2005).

References

Aguilar, Omar, and Mike West. 2000. "Bayesian Dynamic Factor Models and Variance Matrix Discounting For Portfolio Allocation." *Journal of Business and Economic Statistics*, vol. 18, no. 3:338–357.

Alizadeh, Farid, and Donald Goldfarb. 2003. "Second-Order Cone Programming." *Mathematical Programming*, vol. 95, no. 1:3–51.

Armano, G., M. Marchesi, and A. Murru. 2005. "A Hybrid Genetic-Neural Architecture for Stock Indexes Forecasting." *Information Sciences*, vol. 170, no. 1 (February):3–33.

Arrow, Kenneth, and Gerard Debreu. 1954. "Existence of a Competitive Equilibrium for a Competitive Economy." *Econometrica*, vol. 22, no. 3:265–290.

Axtell, Robert. 2001. "Zipf Distribution of U.S. Firm Sizes." *Science*, vol. 293, no. 5536 (September):1818–20.

Banerjee, A., and D.F. Hendry. 1992. "Testing Integration and Cointegration: An Overview." *Oxford Bulletin of Economics and Statistics*, vol. 54, no. 3:225–255.

Barberis, Nicholas, and Richard Thaler. 2003. "A Survey of Behavioral Finance." In *Handbook of the Economics of Finance*. Edited by George Constantinides, Milton Harris, and Rene Stulz. Amsterdam: Elsevier North Holland.

Ben-Tal, Aharon, and Arkadi S. Nemirovski. 1998. "Robust Convex Optimization." *Mathematics of Operations Research*, vol. 23, no. 4:769–805.

———. 1999. "Robust Solutions to Uncertain Linear Programs." *Operations Research Letters*, vol. 25, no. 1:1–13.

———. 2001. *Lectures on Modern Convex Optimization: Analysis, Algorithms, and Engineering Applications*. MPS/SIAM Series on Optimization. Philadelphia, PA: SIAM.

Bernstein, Peter L. 1992. *Capital Ideas: The Improbable Origins of Modern Wall Street*. New York: The Free Press.

———. 1998. *Against the Gods: The Remarkable Story of Risk*. New York: John Wiley & Sons.

Bhargava, Vivek and D.K. Malhotra. Forthcoming 2006. "Do Price-Earnings Ratios Drive Stock Values? Evidence from World Markets." *Journal of Portfolio Management* (Fall).

Black, Fischer, and Robert Litterman. 1990. *Asset Allocation: Combining Investor Views with Market Equilibrium*. Goldman, Sachs & Company, Fixed Income Research (September).

———. 1991. "Global Asset Allocation with Equities, Bonds, and Currencies." Goldman, Sachs & Company, Fixed Income Research.

———. 1992. "Global Portfolio Optimization." *Financial Analysts Journal*, vol. 48, no. 5 (September/October):28–43.

Bodie, Zvi. 1995. "On the Risk of Stock in the Long Run." *Financial Analysts Journal*, vol. 51, no. 3 (May/June):18–22.

Bossaerts. Peter. 1988. "Common Non-Stationary Components of Asset Prices." *Journal of Economic Dynamics and Control*, vol. 12, no. 2/3:348–364.

Breiman, L., J.H. Friedman, R.A. Olshen, and C.J. Stone. 1984. *Classification and Regression Trees*. New York: Chapman and Hall.

Campbell, Harvey R., Kirsten E. Travers, and Michael J. Costa. 2000. "Forecasting Emerging Markets Returns with Neural Networks: A Comparative Study of Nine Emerging Markets." *Emerging Markets Quarterly*, vol. 4, no. 2:43–54.

Campbell, John, Andrew Lo, and Craig A. MacKinlay. 1996. *The Econometrics of Financial Markets*. Princeton, NJ: Princeton University Press.

Campbell, John Y., Martin Lettau, Burton G. Malkiel, and Yexiao Xu. 2001. "Have Individual Stocks Become More Volatile? An Empirical Exploration of Idiosyncratic Risk." *Journal of Finance*, vol. 56, no. 1 (February):1–43.

Canetti, Elias. 1984. *Crowds and Power*. New York: Farrar, Strauss and Giroux.

Choi, J.H., M.K. Lee, and M.V. Rhee. 1995. "Trading S&P 500 Stock Index Futures Using a Neural Network." In *Proceedings of the Third International Conference on Artificial Intelligence Applications on Wall Street*, New York (June).

Cochrane, John H. 1988. "How Big Is the Random Walk in GNP?" *Journal of Political Economy*, vol. 96, no. 5:893–920.

Cybenko, G. 1989. "Approximations by Superpositions of a Sigmoidal Function." *Mathematics of Control Signals & Systems*, vol. 2, no. 4:303–314.

Czyzyk, Joseph, Michael P. Mesnier, and Jorge J. Moré. 1998. "The NEOS Server." *IEEE Journal on Computational Science and Engineering*, vol. 5, no. 3:68–75.

Daconta, Michael C., Leo J. Obrst, and Kevin T. Smith. 2005. *The Semantic Web: A Guide to the Future of XML, Web Services, and Knowledge Management*. Hoboken, NJ: John Wiley & Sons.

Davison, A.C., and D.V. Hinkley. 1999. *Bootstrap Methods and their Applications* Cambridge, U.K.: Cambridge University Press.

DeFusco, Richard A., Dennis W. McLeavey, Jerald E. Pinto, and David E. Runkle. 2004. *Quantitative Methods for Investment Analysis: Second Edition*. Charlottesville, VA: CFA Institute.

El Ghaoui, Laurent, and Herve Lebret. 1977. "Robust Solutions to Least-Squares Problems with Uncertain Data." *SIAM Journal Matrix Analysis with Applications*, vol. 18, no. 4:1035–64.

Engle, Robert F., and Clive W.J. Granger. 1987. "Co-Integration and Error Correction: Representation, Estimation, and Testing." *Econometrica*, vol. 55, no. 2 (March):251–276.

Evans, John L., and Stephen H. Archer. 1968. "Diversification and the Reduction of Dispersion: An Empirical Analysis." *Journal of Finance*, vol. 23, no. 5 (December): 761–767.

Fabozzi, Frank J., Sergio M. Focardi, and Caroline L. Jonas. 2004. "Trends in Quantitative Asset Management in Europe." *Journal of Portfolio Management*, vol. 30, no. 4 (Summer, Special European Section):125–132.

———. 2005. "Market Experience with Modeling for Defined Benefit Pension Funds: Evidence from Four Countries." *Journal of Pension Economics and Finance*, vol. 4, no. 3 (November).

Fabozzi, Frank J., Sergio M. Focardi, and Petter Kolm. 2006a. *Financial Modeling of the Equity Market: From CAPM to Cointegration*. Hoboken, NJ: John Wiley & Sons.

———. Forthcoming 2006b. "A Simple Framework for Time Diversification." *Journal of Investing*.

Falkenberry, Thomas N. 2002. "High Frequency Data Filtering." Tick Data, Inc.

Fama, Eugene F. 1965. "The Behavior of Stock Market Prices." *Journal of Business*, vol. 38, no. 1 (January):34–105.

Fama, Eugene F., and Kenneth. R. French. 1988. "Permanent and Temporary Components of Stock Prices." *Journal of Political Economy*, vol. 96, no. 2 (April):246–273.

————. 1996. "Multifactor Explanations of Asset Pricing Anomalies." *Journal of Finance*, vol. 51, no. 1 (March):55–84.

Fensel, Dieter, Wolfgang Wahlster, Henry Lieberman, and James Hendler. 2004. *Spinning the Semantic Web: Bringing the World Wide Web to Its Full Potential.* Cambridge, MA: MIT Press.

Focardi, Sergio M., and Frank J. Fabozzi. 2004. *The Mathematics of Financial Modeling and Investment Management.* Hoboken, NJ: John Wiley & Sons.

Focardi, Sergio, and Caroline Jonas. 2002. *Leveraging Unstructured Data in Asset Management,* Research Report. Paris: The Intertek Group.

Friedman, Milton. 1953. *Essays in the Theory of Positive Economics.* Chicago, IL: University of Chicago Press.

Goldfarb, Donald, and Garud Iyengar. 2003. "Robust Portfolio Selection Problems." *Mathematics of Operations Research*, vol. 28, no. 1:1–38.

Goldthwaite, Richard A. 1995. *Wealth and the Demand for Art in Italy, 1300–1600.* Baltimore, MD: Johns Hopkins Press.

Gunn, S.R., M. Brown, and K.M. Bossley. 1997. "Network Performance Assessment For Neurofuzzy Data Modelling." In *Intelligent Data Analysis*, vol. 1208 of Lecture Notes in Computer Science. Edited by X. Liu, P. Cohen, and M. Berthold. Berlin: Springer-Verlag.

Hamilton, James D. 1989. "A New Approach to the Economic Analysis of Nonstationary Time Series and the Business Cycle." *Econometrica*, vol. 57, no. 2 (March):357–384.

————. 1996. "Specification Testing in Markov-Switching Time-Series Models." *Journal of Econometrics*, vol. 70, no. 1:127–157.

Harrison, J.M., and D.M. Kreps. 1979. "Martingales and Arbitrage in Multiperiod Securities Markets." *Journal of Economic Theory*, vol. 20, no. 3 (June):381–408.

Harrison, J.M., and S.R. Pliska. 1981. "Martingales and Stochastic Integrals in the Theory of Continuous Trading." *Stochastic Processes and Their Applications*, vol. 11, no. 3:215–260.

————. 1985. "A Stochastic Calculus Model of Continuous Trading: Complete Markets." *Stochastic Processes and Their Applications*, vol. 15, no. 3:313–316.

Hertz, John, Anders Krogh, and Richard G. Palmer. 1991. *Introduction to the Theory of Neural Computation.* Santa Fe Institute Studies in the Sciences of Complexity, Perseus Books Group.

Holland, John. 1976. *Adaptation of Natural and Artificial Systems.* Ann Arbor, MI: University of Michigan.

Hutchinson, James M., Andrew W. Lo, and Tomasio Poggio. 1994. "A Non-Parametric Approach to Pricing and Hedging Derivative Securities via Learning Networks." *Journal of Finance*, vol. 49, no. 3 (July):851–889.

Intertek. 2002. *Leveraging Unstructured Data in Investment Management.* The Intertek Group Paris.

Jegadeesh, Narasimhan, and Sheridan Titman. 1993. "Returns to Buying Winners and Selling Losers: Implications for Stock Market Efficiency." *Journal of Finance*, vol. 48, no. 1 (March):65–91.

———. 2001. "Profitability of Momentum Strategies: An Evaluation of Alternative Explanations." *Journal of Finance*, vol. 56, no. 2 (April):699–720.

Johansen, S. 1991. "Estimation and Hypothesis Testing of Cointegration Vectors in Gaussian Vector Autoregressive Models." *Econometrica*, vol. 59, no. 6 (November): 1551–81.

Kalman, R.E. 1960. "A New Approach to Linear Filtering and Prediction Problems." *Transactions of the ASME—Journal of Basic Engineering*, vol. 82 (Series D):35–45.

Kalman, R.E., and R. Bucy. 1961. "New Results in Linear Filtering and Prediction Theory." *Transactions of the ASME—Journal of Basic Engineering*, vol. 83 (Series D):95–108.

Kanas, Angelos, and Georgios P. Kouretas. 2005. "A Cointegration Approach to the Lead-Lag Effect Among Size-Sorted Equity Portfolios." *International Review of Economics and Finance*, vol. 14, no. 2:181–201.

Kass, G. 1980. "An Exploratory Technique for Investigating Large Quantities of Categorical Data." *Applied Statistics*, vol. 29, no. 2:119–127.

Kazemi, Hossein, Thomas Schneeweis, and Dulari Pancholi. 2003. *Performance Persistence for Mutual Funds: Academic Evidence.* Center for International Securities and Derivatives Markets, University of Massachusetts (May).

Keynes, John Maynard. 1935. *The General Theory of Employment, Interest and Money.* Cambridge, U.K.: Harcourt, Brace and Company.

Kiernan, Vincent. 1994. *The New Scientist*, vol. 5 (December):95–97.

Kim, Myung Jig, Charles R. Nelson, and Richard Startz. 1991. "Mean Reversion in Stock Prices? A Reappraisal of the Empirical Evidence." *Review of Economic Studies*, vol. 58, no. 3 (March):515–528.

Kirman, Alan P. 1994. "Economies with Interacting Agents." Working Paper 94-05-030, Santa Fe Institute.

Koza, John. 1992. *Genetic Programming: On the Programming of Computers by Means of Natural Selection*. Cambridge, MA: The MIT Press.

Kritzman, Mark. 1994. "What Practitioners Need to Know About Time Diversification." *Financial Analysts Journal*, vol. 50, no. 1 (January/February):14–18.

———. 1997. "Time Diversification: An Update." *Economics and Portfolio Strategy*. New York: Peter L. Bernstein, Inc.

Kritzman, Mark, and Don Rich. 2002. "The Mismeasurement of Risk." *Financial Analysts Journal*, vol. 57, no. 3 (May/June):91–99.

Leinweber, David J. 2003. "Delving Deeper." *Bloomberg Wealth Manager*, (November):19–26.

Leinweber, David J., and Yossi Beinart. 1996. "A Little AI Goes a Long Way on Wall Street." *Journal of Portfolio Management*, vol. 27, no. 2 (Winter):95–106.

Leinweber, David J., and Ananth N. Madhavan. 2001. "Three Hundreds Years of Stock Market Manipulations." *Journal of Investing*, vol. 10, no. 2 (Summer):7–16.

LeRoy, S.F. 1973. "Risk Aversion and the Martingale Property of Stock Prices." *International Economic Review*, vol. 14, no. 2 (June):436–446.

Lewellen, Jonathan. 2005. "Temporary Movements in Stock Prices." MIT working paper.

Lintner, John. 1965. "The Valuation of Risk Assets and the Selection of Risky Investments in Stock Portfolios and Capital Budgets." *Review of Economics and Statistics*, vol. 47, no. 1:13–37.

Litterman, Robert B. 1986. "Forecasting With Bayesian Vector Autoregressions— Five Years of Experience." *Journal of Business & Economic Statistics*, vol. 4:25–38.

———. 2003. *Modern Investment Management: An Equilibrium Approach*. Hoboken, NJ: John Wiley & Sons.

Lo, Andrew, and A. Craig MacKinlay. 1988. "Stock Market Prices Do Not Follow Random Walks: Evidence from a Simple Specification Test." *Review of Financial Studies*, vol. 1:41–66.

————. 1990. "When Are Contrarian Profits Due to Stock Market Overreaction?" *Review of Financial Studies*, vol. 3:175–206.

Lobo, Miguel S., Lieyen Vandenberghe, Stephen Boyd, and Herv Lebret. 1998. "Applications of Second-Order Cone Programming." *Linear Algebra and Its Applications*, 284:193–228.

Loh, W., and Y.S. Shih. 1997. "Split Selection Methods for Classification Trees." *Statistica Sinica*, vol. 7, no. 4:815–840.

Loh, W., and N. Vanichestakul. 1988. "Tree-Structured Classification via Generalized Discriminant Analysis." *Journal of American Statistical Association*, vol. 83, no. 403:715–728.

Longford, T. 1993. *Random Coefficient Models.* Oxford, U.K.: Oxford University Press.

Malkiel, Burton. 1973. *A Random Walk Down Wall Street.* New York, NY: W.W. Norton & Co.

————. 2002. "How Much Diversification Is Enough?" In *Equity Portfolio Construction.* Edited by Kathryn Dixon Jost, CFA. Charlottesville, VA: AIMR.

Mandelbrot, Benoît. 1963. "The Variation in Certain Speculative Prices." *Journal of Business*, vol. 36, no. 4:394–419.

Mantegna, Rosario N., and H. Eugene Stanley. 1999. *Introduction to Econophysics: Correlations and Complexity in Finance.* Cambridge: Cambridge University Press.

Markowitz, Harry M. 1952. "Portfolio Selection." *Journal of Finance*, vol. 7, no. 1: 77–91.

————. 1987. *Mean-Variance Analysis in Portfolio Choice and Capital Markets.* Cambridge, MA: Basil Blackwell.

Morgan, J., and R. Messenger. 1973. "A Sequential Analysis Program for the Analysis of Nominal Scale Dependent Variables." Technical Report, University of Michigan.

Mossin, Jan. 1966. "Equilibrium in a Capital Asset Market." *Econometrica*, vol. 34: 768–783.

Mulvey, John M., Koray D. Simsek, Zhuojuan Zhang, Frank J. Fabozzi, and Bill Pauling. 2005. "Assisting Defined-Benefit Pension Plans." Princeton University Report (July).

Muth, John F. 1960. "Optimal Properties of Exponentially Weighted Forecasts." *Journal of the American Statistical* Association, vol. 55, no. 290 (June):299–306.

Nielsen, Steen, and Jan Overgaard Olesen. 2000. "Regime-Switching Stock Returns and Mean Reversion." Working Paper 11–2000, Department of Economics and EPRU, Copenhagen Business School.

Poterba, James, and Lawrence Summers. 1988. "Mean Reversion in Stock Prices: Evidence and Implications." *Journal of Financial Economics*, vol. 79:22–25.

Quinlan, J. Ross. 1979. "Discovering Rules by Induction from Large Collections of Examples." In *Expert Systems in the Micro-Electronic Age*. Edited by Donald Michie. Edinburgh: Edinburgh University Press.

Rachev, Svetlozar T., and Stefan Mittnik. 2000. *Stable Paretian Models in Finance*. Chichester, U.K.: John Wiley & Sons.

Rachev, Svetlozar T., Christian Menn, and Frank J. Fabozzi. 2005. *Fat-Tailed and Skewed Asset Return Distributions: Implications for Risk Management, Portfolio Selection, and Option Pricing*. Hoboken, NJ: John Wiley & Sons.

Refenes, Apostolos-Paul, ed. 1995. *Neural Networks in the Capital Markets*. New York, NY: John Wiley and Sons.

Rhodes, Mark. 2000. *Past Imperfect: the Performance of UK Equity Managed Funds*. Financial Services Authority Occasional Paper (August).

Risager, Ole. 1998. "Random Walk or Mean Reversion: the Danish Stock Market since World War I." Working Paper 7–98, Department of Economics and EPRU, Copenhagen Business School.

Rosenberg, Barr, and James A. Ohlson. 1976. "The Stationary Distribution of Returns and Portfolio Separation in Capital Markets: A Fundamental Contradiction." *Journal of Financial and Quantitative Analysis*, vol. 11, no. 3 (September): 393–401.

Ross, Stephen A. 1976. "The Arbitrage Theory of Capital Asset Pricing." *Journal of Economic Theory*, vol. 13, no. 3 (December):341–360.

Rouwenhorst, K. Geert. 1998. "International Momentum Strategies." *Journal of Finance*, vol. 53, no. 1 (February):267–284.

Samorodnitsky, Gennady, and Murad S. Taqqu. 1994. *Stable Non-Gaussian Processes: Stochastic Models with Infinite Variance*. New York: Chapman and Hall.

Samuelson, Paul A. 1965. "Proof that Properly Anticipated Prices Fluctuate Randomly." *Industrial Management Review*, vol. 6, no. 1 (Spring):41–50.

———. 1994. "The Long-Term Case for Equities." *Journal of Portfolio Management*, vol. 20, no. 1 (Fall):15–24.

Sharpe, William F. 1964. "Capital Asset Prices: A Theory of Market Equilibrium Under Conditions of Risk." *Journal of Finance*, vol. 19, no. 3:425–442.

Simon, Herbert A. 1980. *The New Science of Management Decision*. New York, NY: Harper and Row.

Sorensen, Eric H., Ronald Hua, and Edward Qian. 2005. "Contextual Fundamentals, Models, and Active Management." *Journal of Portfolio Management*, vol. 31, no. 1 (Fall):23–26.

Thawornwong, Suraphan, and David Enke. 2004. "The Adaptive Selection of Financial and Economic Variables for Use with Artificial Neural Networks." *Neurocomputing*, vol. 56:205–232.

Thorley, Steven R. 1995. "The Time-Diversification Controversy." *Financial Analysts Journal*, vol. 51, no. 3 (May/June):68–76.

Tobin, James. 1958. "Liquidity Preferences as Behavior towards Risk." *Review of Economic Studies*, vol. 25, no. 2:65–86.

Treynor, Jack L. 1961. "Towards a Theory of Market Value of Risky Assets." Unpublished manuscript.

Trippi, Robert. 1992. *Neural Networks in Finance and Investing: Using Artificial Intelligence to Improve Real World Performance*. Chicago, IL: Probus Publishing.

Vanini, Paolo, and L. Vignola. 2002. "Optimal Decision-Making with Time Diversification." *European Finance Review*, vol. 6, no. 1:1–30.

Vapnik, Vladimir N. 1995. *The Nature of Statistical Learning Theory*. New York: Springer.

———. 1998. *Statistical Learning Theory*. New York: Springer.

Varian, Hal R. 1992. *Microeconomic Analysis*. New York: W.W. Norton & Co.

Von Neumann, John, and Oskar Morgenstern. 1944. *Theory of Games and Economic Behavior*. Princeton, NJ: Princeton University Press.

Ziemba, William T. 2003. *The Stochastic Programming Approach to Asset, Liability, and Wealth Management*. Charlottesville, VA: Research Foundation of CFA Institute.